Home

Eoin Ó Broin is a TD for Dublin Mid West and Sinn Féin's spokesperson on Housing, Planning and Local Government. He is author of *Matxinada, Basque Nationalism and Radical Basque Youth Movements* (2003) and *Sinn Féin and the Politics of Left Republicanism* (2009).

The World Turned Upside-Down

In 1649, to St. George's Hill
A ragged band they called the Diggers came to show the
people's will
They defied the landlords, they defied the laws
They were the dispossessed reclaiming what was theirs.

We come in peace, they said, to dig and sow.
We come to work the lands in common and to make the waste
ground grow
This earth divided, we will make whole
So it may be a common treasury for all.

The sin of property we do disdain
No man has any right to buy or sell the earth for private gain
By theft and murder they took the land
Now everywhere the walls spring up at their command.

They make the laws to chain us well
The clergy dazzle us with heaven or they damn us into hell
We will not worship the god they serve
The god of greed who feeds the rich while poor folk starve.

We work, we eat together, we need no swords
We will not bow to the masters or pay rent to the lords.
Still we are free though we are poor.
Ye Diggers all stand up for glory, stand up now.

From the men of property the orders came
They sent the hired men and troopers to wipe out the
Diggers' claim
Tear down their cottages, destroy their corn.
They were dispersed – but still the vision lingers on.

You poor take courage, you rich take care
This earth was made a common treasury for everyone to share
All things in common, all people one.
They came in peace – the order came to cut them down.

Words and music © Leon Rosselson, 1975

The lyrics are derived from a seventeenth-century pamphlet
attributed to the English Digger leader Gerrard Winstanley.

Home

Why Public
Housing is
the Answer

Eoin Ó Broin

MERRION
PRESS

Democratic Programme
Adopted by Dáil Éireann 21.1.1919

We declare in the words of the Irish Republican Proclamation the right of the people of Ireland to the ownership of Ireland, and to the unfettered control of Irish destinies to be indefeasible, and in the language of our first President, Pádraig Mac Phiarais, we declare that the Nation's sovereignty extends not only to all men and women of the Nation, but to all its material possessions, the Nation's soil and all its resources, all the wealth and all the wealth-producing processes within the Nation, and with him we reaffirm that all right to private property must be subordinated to the public right and welfare.

We declare that we desire our country to be ruled in accordance with the principles of Liberty, Equality, and Justice for all, which alone can secure permanence of Government in the willing adhesion of the people.

We affirm the duty of every man and woman to give allegiance and service to the Commonwealth, and declare it is the duty of the Nation to assure that every citizen shall have opportunity to spend his or her strength and faculties in the service of the people. In return for willing service, we, in the name of the Republic, declare the right of every citizen to an adequate share of the produce of the Nation's labour.

It shall be the first duty of the Government of the Republic to make provision for the physical, mental and spiritual well-being of the children, to secure that no child shall suffer hunger or cold from lack of food, clothing, or shelter, but that all shall be provided with the means and facilities requisite for their proper education and training as Citizens of a Free and Gaelic Ireland.

The Irish Republic fully realises the necessity of abolishing the present odious, degrading and foreign Poor Law System, substituting therefor a sympathetic native scheme for the care of the Nation's aged and infirm, who shall not be regarded as a burden, but rather entitled to the Nation's gratitude and consideration. Likewise it shall be the duty of the Republic to take such measures as will safeguard the health of the people and ensure the physical as well as the moral well-being of the Nation.

It shall be our duty to promote the development of the Nation's resources, to increase the productivity of its soil, to exploit its mineral deposits, peat bogs, and fisheries, its waterways and harbours, in the interests and for the benefit of the Irish people.

It shall be the duty of the Republic to adopt all measures necessary for the recreation and invigoration of our Industries, and to ensure their being developed on the most beneficial and progressive co-operative and industrial lines. With the adoption of an extensive Irish Consular Service, trade with foreign Nations shall be revived on terms of mutual advantage and goodwill, and while undertaking the organisation of the Nation's trade, import and export, it shall be the duty of the Republic to prevent the shipment from Ireland of food and other necessaries until the wants of the Irish people are fully satisfied and the future provided for.

It shall also devolve upon the National Government to seek co-operation of the Governments of other countries in determining a standard of Social and Industrial Legislation with a view to a general and lasting improvement in the conditions under which the working classes live and labour.

First published in 2019 by
Merrion Press
An imprint of Irish Academic Press
10 George's Street
Newbridge
Co. Kildare
Ireland
www.merrionpress.ie

9781785372650 (Paper)
9781785372667 (Kindle)
9781785372674 (Epub)
9781785372681 (PDF)

British Library Cataloguing in Publication Data
An entry can be found on request

Library of Congress Cataloging in Publication Data
An entry can be found on request

Typeset in Classical Garamond BT 11/15 pt

Cover front and back: Architect: 24H-architecture, Rotterdam;
Boris Zeisser and Maartje Lammers.
Copyright images: Boris Zeisser.
Back-cover photo of the author by Mark Nixon,
www.marknixon.com.

All royalties from this book will be donated to
Inner City Helping Homeless.

Contents

Coda

Acknowledgements

To Lynn … for everything but mainly for putting up with me.

To Ailbhe, for advice, assistance and patience.

To Iñaki, Maite, Mikel & Irati for poking fun at my procrastination (oh yeah and the great company).

To Izei for the voice message … maitia idatzi dut.

To Cooper, because if I don't Lynn won't speak to me.

To *Bóthar Buí* (Sarah & Kieran) for space to think and inspiration to write (oh yeah and the amazing shrimp).

To Peter O'Connell for good advice and even better contacts.

To Conor, Fiona and all the team at Merrion Press for making the impossible happen.

And to Adrienne in MacCarthy's bar Castletownbere for the Hewitts Whisky.

To the significant number of housing policy analysts, practitioners, public servants, activists and constituents whose experiences, writings and conversations have given me a wealth of knowledge on which the words that follow are based.

To Michelle, Simon, Nicola, Frank and Paul for comments on the draft.

Deficiencies and Terminology

The original intention of this book was to address the Irish housing system in its entirety, i.e. in both the South and North of Ireland. Unfortunately, due to limitations in my own knowledge, time and space I have had to reduce the focus to just the housing system in Southern Ireland. Throughout the book the term South of Ireland refers to the entity officially known as the Republic of Ireland. Given that I am a Sinn Féin TD and committed Irish republican I doubt you need me to explain the rationale for this.

Preface

Paul Mason

Over the past thirty years, Governments all across the world began to insert market mechanisms and market norms of behaviour into many parts of society where they do not exist.

Where there was resistance, they did it by force. Bus and train services that were once run in the public interest were forced to 'compete' with each other; so were schools, universities, even the people who serve school dinners and clean the offices.

At the same time, more and more of us were forced to behave as if we were a tiny, individual bank. We were taught to evaluate our success not just through our wages and what they can buy but through the 'assets' we own, and the numerous lines of credit we could command.

These two relentless forces – marketisation and financialisation – formed the core dynamics of a strategy known as neoliberalism. A third dynamic – globalisation – made us prey to the avarice of rich elites across the world, not just our homegrown ones; and forced us to compete in a labour market that begins at the local bus stop and ends at a bus stop in Shanghai.

As a result, in the space of two generations housing got transformed into a weapon in the hands of globalised finance.

This is how it works. If you can constrain the supply of something, the price of it should go up. With housing that means constraining the supply of land and buildings.

But if, at the same time, you put unlimited supplies of cheap money into the hands of people who already have money, something unusual happens. Land is acquired, apartment blocks are built – but the prices seldom fall. Because property has become a one-way bet.

The price of a home no longer responds to the supply and demand of buildings but the supply and demand for money.

As long as Central Banks operate a cheap money policy – whether to encourage speculation as before 2008 or to keep the economy on life support as after 2008 – the chances are that property prices rise faster than incomes and rents.

Since 2015, Ireland is second only to Canada in the developed world when it comes to house prices rising faster than incomes, and high up the global league table when it comes to rents:

https://www.imf.org/external/research/housing/.

If you add in the boom for speculative commercial property building, the picture in many cities and large towns across the developing world is of a frantic building boom and a shortage of affordable places to live. The housing market no longer responds to human need, but to the rhythms of finance.

Supporters of free-market economics insist this outcome is natural and spontaneous. In fact it is the result of relentless coercion and intervention by the State. The rundown terraced house, with every room turned into a bedroom; the ex-council flat turned into an Airbnb while people huddle under sleeping bags in doorways; the lights-off apartment blocks, bought off-plan and left empty by some footballer or crook. We walk past the evidence every day.

Periodically it all goes bust, and some bankers flee the country, and some politicians are disgraced and people on radio phone-ins get shouty.

But then the State steps in, in the form of the Central Bank, saves the speculators and floods the market with more cheap money, pricing ordinary people out of affordable homes some more.

The only thing that's going to break this cycle is political action by the State. In the first place, it's a question of separating the market for housing from the market for financial assets.

You can place limits on foreign buyers. That means limiting the forces of globalisation that are worshipped with a religious zeal in politics; they will call it protectionism. But it is just protecting families, communities and social cohesion.

You can cap rents. That means limiting the power of finance – because rents are always set exactly at what the lenders to landlords need, not what renters can afford. They will say it's impossible, and that it never works. Ask the rack-renting landlords of New York City why they devote years to ejecting tenants with capped rents: it works.

You can enforce a quota of affordable homes for buying and renting in every new private development. If you study the way developers systematically erode these quotas, once they've got planning permission, you can see how effective they might be.

But ultimately, the most important action the State must take is to build homes for social rent. It has to plan them, build them, own them, hold on to them and manage the allocation according to the most pressing need. It needs to build so rapidly that who gets what becomes a non-issue.

Across the western world, after the Second World War, where the private sector could not provide decent homes, the State did. As Ó Broin points out in this book, under Bevan the British Labour Government initiated a housebuilding programme explicitly premised on the idea of housing as a public good, not a commodity.

This time around we face different challenges to those that confronted the post-war generation. People are flocking to big cities – not just the young but the elderly – after a life of farming or small-town manufacturing.

More people want to live singly – or in shared accommodation. The rise of networked lifestyles has socialised many aspects of urban living, from Starbucks to the gym – so that what people want from the space they live in might be changing. There is also the challenge of meeting tough targets on carbon use and circularity (inbuilt recyclability).

The biggest mistake would be to look at the current state of the built environment and see it as the product of randomness plus demographic change. It is the precise outcome of planned action by the rich against the poor.

From the slums of Manila, built alongside the sewers, to depopulated cities in the American Rust Belt like Gary, Indiana; to places like Barcelona, whose social fabric is being destroyed by Airbnb – I've reported the way neoliberalism has massively redrawn the map of human dwelling patterns. The lesson I take from it is: it can all be redrawn again, this time with the people in control.

In this hard-hitting and timely book, Ó Broin exposes the failures in politics and economics that plunged Ireland into a housing crisis. He also argues that change lies in the hands of a new generation of politicians and activists, and the question they face is this: are we to see homes as places to generate rent and interest from, or as places to live?

Paul Mason is a British journalist and author of the book *Postcapitalism: A Guide to our Future*

Overture

Inadequate Language

Every day our attention is drawn to housing. Homelessness has reached record highs. Thousands of children are spending years living in unsuitable and overcrowded emergency accommodation. Tens of thousands of people are unable to access appropriate, secure and affordable housing. Rents and house prices continue to rise while an entire generation of young people are locked out of the private market. Social housing delivery is glacial, waiting lists are too long and rent subsidy dependence is growing. The private sector is building too few homes at the wrong price. Accidental landlords are leaving the market and are being replaced by vulture funds.

Increasing numbers of people are affected by and concerned with the failures of our housing system. In newspapers, television shows, casual conversations or arguments in pubs and parliaments, housing is the topic of the moment. But how adequate is the language we are using to describe what is happening around us?

We talk of 'market failure' as if the provision of housing operated inside some kind of private sector bubble free from State intervention. The word 'failure' suggests either a lack of success or a problem caused by the omission of some required action that never took place.

We use the word 'broken' suggesting that our housing system once worked but has at some point in its development fragmented into pieces. The word describes something that was badly designed or poorly implemented. But also something that with the right intervention could be put back together again.

More and more we talk of 'crisis' as instability, trauma and hardship increasingly come to describe people's experiences of trying to access secure and affordable accommodation. For some, 'crisis' also speaks of a crucial or decisive turning point, a sudden change of course or, in drama, a high point immediately preceding the resolution of a conflict. For others, 'crisis' is the inevitable outworking of the cycles of the market economy as boom turns to bust, only to repeat itself endlessly.

In response, reformers ponder how best to ameliorate, but not eradicate, the worst impacts of this unavoidable sequence of events while revolutionaries agitate for some imagined rupture and new beginning.

Some prefer the word 'emergency' both because it speaks to the immediate risks facing so many people while at the same time demanding urgent attention and greater intervention to get the 'crisis' under control. But 'emergency' also sounds like an accident that requires you to be rushed to your local hospital. These 'emergency' departments never go away, they just see different people on different days with different 'emergencies' without end.

Others talk of 'scandal', 'disaster' or 'catastrophe'. The first suggests something that offends or causes reputational damage, presumably of those responsible. The second and third imply an unforeseen event, something natural possibly, maybe even on a greater scale than originally imagined.

For me none of these words work. They fail to fully grasp what is going on around us. Housing is not a purely 'market' activity and the State, past and present, is intimately involved in every aspect of its financing, building, pricing and allocation.

And surely 'market failure' is a tautology. Allowing the market too much of a role in the provision of housing is always destined to fail. History, if nothing else, teaches us that.

Indeed, talking about 'market failure' suggests that it has an opposite called 'market success'. Such a thing may exist for the few, but it definitely does not exist for the many.

Housing is a system involving both State and market. There are also non-governmental, academic and media agents whose role is important. And crucially there are real people not just living in, or seeking to live in, but financing, planning, building, pricing, allocating and paying for the places they come to call home.

Our housing system never worked properly. It was never in a fixed or whole state only to be broken and fragmented somewhere along the way.

It certainly is in crisis but whether this is a key moment in the creation of something better is not yet clear. And are we really consigned to the Hobson's choice of an inadequate amelioration or an impossible revolution?

For tens of thousands of families and individuals the inability to access secure and affordable accommodation certainly is an emergency demanding urgent action but was this really an accident, the result of a bad fall or clumsily decision?

And of course what is going on in housing today is a scandal but I wonder if those responsible are really suffering any repetitional damage. Unfortunately, too many people think of the hardship they see around them as the result of some natural disaster or human catastrophe, a localised problem rather than a system failure.

Each of these words describe a piece of our housing problem but none of them quite get to the root of the meaning of what we are living through. This is not just about semantics. Words matter. How we describe what we see in our society is in effect how we diagnose the problem we want to solve. Bad diagnosis can lead to bad treatment with the patient never recovering.

The word I would choose to describe our housing system is dysfunctional. The Greek origin of the word connotes something 'bad', 'abnormal' or 'difficult'. The Latin root speaks to a 'lack' of something. In more recent times the word means an abnormality or impairment in an organ or system. But it has also come to describe the disruption of normal social relations.

This gets to the very heart of the matter. Housing is not just a physical thing, the bricks and mortar, timber and steel within which we live. It is a relationship between the providers and the occupiers, between the State and the market, between people who create homes for families who in turn create communities.

A functioning housing system is one in which all people have access to safe, secure and affordable accommodation to meet their needs. It is a system in which everyone has a place they can call home.

Of course, our current housing system functions for some, those who have access to a home. Nor is there any doubt that there are those who benefit from the dysfunction, whose profit is dependent on the system being perpetually bad, abnormal and difficult. But for many, indeed globally for the majority, accessing safe, secure and affordable accommodation is uncertain and is certainly a struggle.

Today in Ireland, and across much of the world, our housing system is completely dysfunctional. It is bad, abnormal and difficult. More importantly these negative experiences for millions of people are the result of abnormal and impaired relationships between the key players in the system. And these are damaging wider social relationships, creating hardship, insecurity, fear and anger.

If you believe, as I do, that good-quality, safe, secure, appropriate and affordable accommodation should be for the many not just the few then understanding the way in which these relationships have become abnormal and impaired during the course of the modern history of housing provision is crucial if solutions are to be found.

Real People

Of course words, no matter how descriptive or evocative, cannot fully capture the lived reality of housing stress facing tens of thousands of families and individuals. Every single day, ever growing numbers of people find accessing secure and affordable accommodation difficult if not impossible.

This book is motivated by their stories and is written in an attempt to help solve the problems they face.

Una and Sean

Una is a full-time mother. Her partner Sean has a badly paid job. They used to live in private rented accommodation with their five children until the landlord raised the rent to an impossible level. In the two years before receiving their Notice to Quit rents had increased 20 percent.

They presented to the Council's homeless desk. With only nine years on the housing list they still had two years to go before an allocation. All the desk clerk could offer them was hotel accommodation on the other side of the city.

Every morning they would leave the hotel at 6.30am and take the two-hour bus journey to drop the kids to school. Each starting at a different time. Sean would head off to work while Una would wander the streets waiting for collection time, staggered from 2.30 to 4.30pm.

Then they would make the long bus journey back to the hotel, tired and cranky, stuck in rush hour traffic.

The hotel room was clean but there was no place to cook or to store their stuff. Homework was a nightmare with all five children trying to read and write sprawled out on the large double bed. Health and safety meant the children couldn't leave the room unattended. It was suffocating.

And then there were the arguments. The children's behaviour started to change. Una's relationship with Sean was under real strain. There was no advice, no help, nowhere to turn to. Sure they could have talked to friends or family but the shame of not being able to provide for their children forced them to put a brave face on their daily struggles.

Looking back it is hard to believe that they lasted the full fourteen months. When the call came from the Council with an allocation in Una's old estate it was like a million Christmases came at once. The joy in the children's eyes was indescribable.

They have moved in now and their routine is back to normal. But Una can see the difference in the family. The youngest one is more introverted. The eldest more bold.

And Sean, well he doesn't say much but he still hasn't gotten over the shame of it all.

Laura

Laura and her young twins live in the box bedroom of her mother's Council house. To be honest, box is an overstatement. Between her bed, the bunk-beds for the girls and all the kids' things there is literally no space to move.

Her mam and dad have the main bedroom. Her sister has the other bedroom. And her brother sleeps on the couch. Laura doesn't recall the house feeling so cramped when she was growing up.

She remembers when the babies were born. Their father was so happy. He promised he would have the deposit for a flat saved in a few months and that Laura could decorate it whatever way she wanted. They knew it would be a long wait for a Council house but that didn't matter. His job wasn't bad and the prospect of more hours was good.

The babies were just 18 months old when the crash happened. They never caught the driver of the car that caused the accident but the CCTV clearly showed they were drunk, careering down the wrong side of the road. The damage from the crash was so bad Laura never got to see his body.

She cried for a month. Only the twins kept her going. Sure she had to hold it together for them. But now the girls were six. Six long years trapped in the box bedroom.

Laura has been to every TD and Councillor and they all tell her the same thing. The waiting time for a two bedroom is eleven years long. Without medical or homeless priority she just has to wait it out. The idea of another five years cooped up in the box bedroom is hard to face.

The damp started to appear after the girls turned four. Big black patches in the corners and around the window sills. Laura is convinced it is making the girls' asthma worse. The Council say it's condensation and she should open the windows more often. Are they serious? It's cold enough in here what with the old rotten wooden window frames. She's not sure which is worse, the damp musty smell of the mould or the sharp stink of bleach that hangs in the room for days after the weekly clean.

Five more years. The girls will be eleven before they have a place they can call home. But then at least she's not stuck in some grotty BnB in the city centre. The girl across the road was almost two years homeless. At least she has her family and friends around her. But still ... five more years ...

John

John was employed all his life with the Corporation. He was an honest and hard-working man. He and his wife bought the family home in the 1970s. A beautiful semi-detached house in one of the new private estates. The kids were born. Wages were good. He was happy. Until the drink took hold.

He doesn't remember how long it took but the marriage eventually broke down. He left the house and got digs in the city centre. Eventually he dried out and got his life back together. But too late to patch things up at home. That part of his life was gone forever.

He managed to keep his job. Sober for ten years, he secured a promotion and life went on. His landlord was a decent man. Charged a fair rent, kept the flat in good order, never intruded.

But now John is retired, his pension is small and the landlord is selling up. He couldn't believe it when he saw what the market rents were for a small one bedroom flat, €1,200 a month! The Housing Assistance Payment (HAP) would cover just half that. His pension brings in €897.43 a month. So after rent he would be left with just €297 a month to live on. Impossible!

The Council might be able to offer him something but not for a few years. What will he do until then? At his age he couldn't face a hostel full of drug users. Nothing wrong with them mind you, but not at his age. Maybe he'll find a bedsit in the city centre. They were banned a few years back but he's heard there are still a few on offer. The prospect of an outside toilet up a flight of stairs at his age and with his enlarged prostate gland is pretty daunting.

John has six months before his Notice to Quit comes up. Something will come up. Maybe his landlord will change his mind. But to be honest at 70 years of age he never thought he would be facing this.

Other real people

These are not fictional stories. They are real cases from my constituency clinic. And there are thousands more.

I could tell you about the student who may have to leave college midway through his degree in business management because the rent is so high after a 17 percent increase, the third such hike in three years. Even with his part-time job he can't manage. He could commute but the five-hour round trip every day would have a real impact on his studies. Maybe he should just pack it in and get a job. The local supermarket in his home village is looking for full-time staff. Who knows, after a few months there might even be a supervisor's role.

Then there is the young graduate, working hard in her first job having to choose between paying for rent, fuel or food as payday approaches. A while back the cooker broke but the landlord took a month to fix it. Living on takeaways for four weeks straight is no joke. She could have taken him to the Residential Tenancies Board but flats are so scarce these days she didn't want to risk being hit with a Notice to Quit.

Or the working couple in their thirties desperate to save a deposit to buy their own home, forced to live apart because there isn't enough space in either of their parents' houses for both of them. When there are young children involved the separation is even more painful. And because house prices are so damn high, even when they have the deposit securing the mortgage is not guaranteed. They could always look for somewhere outside the city. What a choice; never-ending commutes or impossible mortgage payments.

I could take you to Traveller halting sites where families are living in Dickensian conditions which should have been eradicated in the nineteenth century. I could introduce you to families with special needs children living in accommodation that is so unsuitable it is actively holding back their physical and emotional development. I could bring you to Direct Provision centres where families who have secured their legal right to remain in the country are trapped in their hotel room for years because they cannot secure private rental accommodation.

These are the human faces of our dysfunctional housing system. They are people who are doing everything right. They get up early in the morning. They work hard. They care for their children. They respect their neighbours. All they want is the chance to have a place to call home. But our housing system is so bad, abnormal and difficult they simply can't access secure and affordable accommodation.

In the pages that follow there will be a lot of facts and statistics. But behind every single number stands Una and Sean and their five children, Laura and her twins, John, struggling students, hard pressed renters, delayed first-time buyers, those living on the absolute fringes of our housing system and tens of thousands like them. Victims of a housing system that is abnormal, impaired and disruptive of normal social relations.

A Dysfunctional System

Why is our housing system like this? Was it always this way? What decisions were made, or not made, and by whom, that resulted in such dysfunction? Does it have to be this way? What alternatives are there? How much would they cost? How long would they take to implement? What do we have to do to get those in power to listen and act? Do we have to take power ourselves to make the necessary changes?

These are the questions that I will try to answer in the pages that follow. In asking and hopefully answering them I am trying to achieve a number of things. Firstly, to fully understand why we are where we are today. Secondly, to describe what a functional housing system could look like. And thirdly to set out a plan of action for all those who believe, as I do, that change can only be achieved through mass social mobilisation and progressive parliamentary action.

My central argument is that our housing system is this way because it was designed so. People in positions of power took advice and made decisions which resulted in the dysfunction all around us. Sometimes they did so with sincere and genuine intent. Other times they were incompetent, corrupt or greedy. But what matters is less why people made these decisions, more the impact those decisions had and continue to have on the lives of real people.

The key features of our current housing system are an under-provision of public non-market housing and an over-reliance on the private market to meet housing need. This involves massive subsidies to landowners, developers, landlords and investment funds. It is based on a conception of housing as a commodity rather than a social necessity. It prioritises, whether intentionally or not, profit over need and as a consequence generates levels of housing inequality and poverty which are structural requisites rather than unintended consequences of the system.

Any alternative functional housing system must reverse these trends and place the large-scale provision of public non-market housing at its very centre. Housing is too fundamental a need for human well-being to be left to the boom and bust cycle of the market.

The book that follows attempts to make the argument, in as convincing a manner as possible, that at the core of our dysfunctional housing system is an over-reliance on the private market and thus the key ingredient to a stable, secure and affordable housing system is public housing.

But slogans and sound bites are not enough. The people in need of safe, secure and affordable housing deserve more than that. They need a credible, costed and coherent alternative to our current dysfunctional housing system. One that can be implemented in the real world, that can secure the active endorsement of a majority of the people and that with the right kind of Government could start to be constructed from today.

Somewhere between the sincerity of inadequate amelioration and the energy of impossibilist rupture lies a pathway to a functional housing system that guarantees all people a place they can call home. The book you are about to read tries to signpost that pathway and offer a glimpse, albeit sketchy, of the final destination.

Movement 1

The State Gets Involved

Modern Housing

The formation of the Land League in 1879 marks the beginning of the social movement for modern housing in Ireland. It is no accident that Michael Davitt's first-hand account of this turning point in our national history is titled *The Fall of Feudalism in Ireland*.

The demands of this powerful national network of tenant farmers was to shape the State's response to housing need in the decades that followed. In turn these changes, in both urban and rural Ireland, laid the foundations for the housing system that was to develop during the course of the twentieth century.

Midway through the nineteenth century 80 percent of the population of Ireland lived in dwellings made of mud on land rented from landlords. Half of these comprised single-room huts with no windows in which families and animals lived, ate and slept together. The other half had more rooms and usually windows but could still only be described as basic.[1]

The remaining 20 percent were divided between those living in farmhouses or small urban homes with more than five rooms and windows, and the very wealthy 2 percent of society who lived in absolute luxury whether in the big country houses or Georgian city homes.[2]

The Great Hunger from 1845, between starvation and emigration, wiped out huge swathes of the rural population. In the decade up to 1851 the number of single room mud cabins fell by a dramatic 355,689 or 71 percent of the pre-famine total.[3] Alongside the swelling numbers of people in graveyards and coffin ships, the famine saw a dramatic shift of people to the cities and towns.

The intolerable conditions of the rural poor sparked decades of agrarian protest, first in the form of localised societies such as Whiteboys and Ribbonmen. Aggrieved at maltreatment by landlords and their agents these secret organisations took their revenge in the dead of night, maiming or driving cattle, damaging property or, worse still, taking life.

The rage of rural Ireland found expression in the writings of radicals such as James Fintan Lalor during the 1840s, Charles Gavin Duffy's Tenant Right League of the 1850s and the failed Fenian rebellion of 1867.

But it was the Land League founded by former Fenian Michael Davitt with the support of leading nationalist politicians including Charles Stewart Parnell that galvanised these disparate expressions of discontent into a truly national movement.

The league combined mass meetings, boycotts and rent strikes in its campaign to improve the lot of tenant farmers and ultimately to secure the abolition of landlordism. While opposed to violence, agrarian reprisals against landlords continued to form part of the backdrop of what was to become known as the Land War.

The movement went beyond the calls for fair rent, fixity of tenure and free sale, arguing that the land issue could only be finally resolved through widescale tenant proprietorship. This core demand became the focus of a four-year campaign during which the Land League opposed evictions and rent increases while attempting to secure legislative reform in Westminster.

Concerned by the rising levels of political and social agitation, the British Government eventually responded with a series of land reforms which over the next decades redistributed huge tracts of rural Ireland from landlords to tenant farmers.

The Kilmainham Treaty settlement between Parnell and Gladstone may have demobilised the movement and angered the radicals, Davitt included, but its outcome was to prove as important to the development of Irish society in the twentieth century as many of the better known historical events.

Land Reform and Rural Housing

While the 1870 Landlord and Tenant (Ireland) Act sought to quell the rising tide of rural protest, its measures were weak and outpaced by events. It was not until the 1881 Land Act that real reform got underway. In the two decades that followed, seven significant pieces of land legislation passed through Westminster.[4]

The Land Act increased tenants' security of tenure, established a Land Court to deal with disputes and fix rents for fifteen-year terms, and set up a Land Commission backed with loans to assist a tenant purchase scheme. This was followed by the 1882 Arrears of Rent (Ireland) Act which gave grants to 100,000 tenants to clear their arrears, a condition of access to both the Land Court and Commission.

The year 1885 brought in the Purchase of Land (Ireland) Act providing the equivalent of €5 million in long-term loans for tenant purchase with a second round of loans to the same value provided for in the 1887 Land Purchase Act. The 1891 Land Purchase Act provided the equivalent of a further €33 million in 100 percent loans followed in 1903 with another round of loans repayable over sixty-eight years. Compulsory acquisition powers were granted in the 1909 Land Act specifically to relieve congestion.

Padraic Kenna notes that prior to the enactment of this raft of legislation '13,000 landlords owned and controlled the whole rural area of Ireland' while by 1920 '316,000 holdings were purchased by tenants on some 11.5 million acres ... Some 750,000 acres were also distributed to 35,000 allottees, and 10,000 holdings were created from intermixed or rundale lands, mainly through the Congested Districts Board.'[5]

Alongside land reform, political pressure from the Land League and Irish Parliamentary Party in Westminster forced the Government to introduce a series of Labourers Acts in 1883, 1885, 1891 and 1896. These provided loans for the provision of rural cottages for farmers. There were 16,000 such cottages constructed by 1900 with a total of 36,000 provided for by 1914. In many instances the State subsidised the loans used by labourers to purchase these dwellings by as much as 36 percent.[6]

The legacy of the Land League was to transform land ownership in Ireland to such an extent that half a million rural families became private land- and homeowners. It undoubtedly improved the quality of life for those involved, giving them permanent security of tenure over their homes and farming livelihoods. In the 1840s just 17 percent of tenant farmers lived in houses with five or more rooms. By 1901 the number had increased to a dramatic 56 percent.[7] By 1911 just 1 percent of tenant farmers lived in what was then classified as fourth class dwellings.[8] However, inequalities in access to secure and affordable accommodation persisted.

Landless labourers benefited little if at all from this massive redistribution. While their numbers declined by more than half during the final decades of the nineteenth century, they remained a significant presence in rural Ireland. However, their campaigning demands were more often than not for better wages rather than improved housing and their future in many instances lay in migration into the towns and cities. And it was here that the real inequalities in housing conditions were to be found.

Urban Housing

Cathal O'Connell notes that an 1861 Dublin Corporation report found a third of all houses within the city boundary were tenements.[9] Fifty thousand people lived in just 8,000 dwellings in 'fetid and poisonous conditions'. A flood of destitute migrants from the countryside followed the years of famine as Cork, Limerick and smaller towns saw their populations swell.

The immediate response was the public inquiry where Government bodies or philanthropic societies studied the conditions of the urban poor: 1865 saw the creation of Dublin Corporation's Public Health Committee with its first report published the following year; 1880 saw the publication of the Commission of Inquiry into sewage and drainage in Dublin, with a Royal Commission of Inquiry into Working Class Housing five years later; 1900 saw a report on high mortality rates in Dublin with a second report on the same subject six years later.

The 1885 Royal Commission found 32,000 families living in just 7,200 houses in Dublin. Almost 60 percent of the city's population was living in tenements. Meanwhile 22,000 people were crammed into 1,731 tenement buildings in Cork.

This substantial body of evidence confirmed time and again the squalid conditions of the urban working class. Chronic overcrowding, debilitating poverty, disease and high adult and infant mortality were widespread. Private landlords, driven by greed, had no qualms about putting their tenants' lives, let alone health and safety, at risk.

In response, Government passed the Labouring Classes (Lodging Houses and Dwellings) Act in 1866 providing loans to cover half the cost of providing housing for the poor. Take up was limited. Some philanthropic societies and private companies did enter the fray. The Dublin Artisans Dwellings Company was founded in 1876 by prominent businesspeople to house the poor. Through a mixture of private loans and State subsidies it provided 3,600 homes.[10]

Other prominent providers included the Industrial Tenements Company, the Peabody Trust, the Guinness Trust and the Sutton Housing Trust. While some were purely commercial enterprises others had a social reforming zeal. The Iveagh Trust, which still houses social tenants in Dublin's Liberties today, is possibly the best known of these, combining housing with baths, markets and social activities for children focused on educational and moral improvement.

In the main, however, output was low and the housing was aimed at better-paid artisans rather than the worst off of the urban poor. By 1908 just 5,000 urban dwellings had been provided. The tenement problem in Dublin at the start of the twentieth century was considerably worse than other cities. An estimated 36 percent of families were living in single rooms in the capital compared to 15 percent in London and just 1 percent in Cork and Belfast.[11] The result was that Dublin had the highest infant mortality rate in Britain and Ireland as half of the city's population continued to live in insanitary and overcrowded tenements.[12]

According to Diarmaid Ferriter, in 1911 '66% of Dublin's working-class population of 128,000 were deemed to be living in substandard housing' while 118,000 people were crammed into 5,000 tenement buildings.[13]

As with the rural poor, housing conditions in urban Ireland only began to change when anger turned into protest. Public awareness of the plight of the urban poor was raised following the launch of a new social policy periodical *Studies* in 1912 which devoted significant space to covering the housing issue. The collapse of two tenement buildings in Church Street, central Dublin in 1913, killing seven people, provoked widespread anger. Set against the backdrop of rising trade union militancy during the Lockout of the same year it was only a matter of time before organised labour focused its attention on the housing conditions of working people.

During the 1914 local elections the Labour Party in Dublin campaigned under the slogan 'Vote for Labour, Sweep away the Slums'.[14] In the same year the Irish Trades Union Congress passed a motion demanding 'legislation to secure ... the building of healthy homes for all'.[15]

The result of all of this awareness raising and agitation was the setting up of the Dublin Housing Inquiry which criticised some property-owning members of the Corporation for displaying 'little sense of their responsibilities as landlords'. The report found that 60,000 people were in immediate need of housing and recommended the provision of 100 percent loans to fund urban housing for the poor and the conversion of tenements into proper accommodation.

Demonstrating the prevailing pro landlord attitude in some circles at the time Ferriter, commenting on a 1917 article in *Studies* by a medical doctor dealing with the relationship between poor health and bad housing, notes that

> It was revealing that he [the author] believed many would see as 'revolutionary' the suggestion that no person should be allowed to derive profit from a house unless the house was in good sanitary condition and in good habitable repair.[16]

A needs assessment carried out under the terms of The Housing (Ireland) Act 1919 estimated a requirement of 61,648 houses for the urban working class. Local Authorities submitted proposals to provide 42,000 of these to be delivered by 1922.

But the War of Independence and Civil War intervened and the plans were never realised. The challenge of addressing the housing needs of the urban working classes would have to wait until after partition and the creation of two separate States on the island of Ireland.[17]

Why was the Land League more successful at securing improvements in rural Ireland than their urban counterparts in the labour movement?

The obvious answer is that Ireland was still a predominantly rural country with a majority of the population and thus political power resting outside of the larger cities.

In addition to this, the Land League was more intimately connected with the struggle, first for Home Rule and later for Independence, in a way that the labour movement was not. The relatively apolitical nature of craft unionism at the end of the nineteenth century, before the arrival of the more radical general unions, left organised labour at a distance from the national movement.

The strength of Belfast-based municipal socialism and its ties to both Unionist politics and the British labour movement divided the trade union movement during these crucial years, further weakening its strength both with the emerging nationalist political class in Westminster and with the predominant landlord interests that were to lead Northern Unionism post-partition.

Urban Ireland, north and south, would have to wait some decades before the State would start to respond to its housing needs as it had done for rural Ireland.

Free State – The First Decade

Fiscal conservatism and a reluctance to intervene to address acute housing need was to dominate the newly established Government in Dublin post-partition. Richard Mulcahy, the Minister for Local Government, made his views clear when in 1929 he told Dáil Éireann that 'the State cannot bear on its shoulders the burden of solving this particular problem'. While his Ministerial colleague Patrick McGilligan was more blunt stating that 'people may have to die in this country and die of starvation'.[18]

Despite the widespread housing need across the country and in particular the appalling conditions in urban housing in Dublin, Cork and other urban centres, the Government seemed unwilling or unable to tackle the problem.

The politics of housing in the new Free State from 1922 to 1931 was dominated by the same priorities as pre-independence. Rural housing took precedence over urban provision. Subsidies for private homeownership outstripped the provision of publicly owned accommodation. Meanwhile ongoing concern about the poor quality of life in tenement slums failed to provoke a significant State response.

However, new dynamics also emerged including disputes over whether the responsibility for addressing housing need lay with Central or Local Government and the question of whether relationships between builders, landlords and politicians were conducive to or corrupting of good housing policy.

The 1922 million pound fund led to the building of 2,000 public houses in urban areas such as Marino, Dublin. Modelled on the Garden City concept in vogue in Britain at the time the scheme sought to build good quality homes for artisan workers in steady employment. The standards were indeed high, as were the rents, excluding those in less secure or lower paid employment.

The failure to invest in housing for the poor provoked criticism, not just from the opposition benches, but from the Government party as well. During an adjournment debate on housing in May 1923 the influential pro Treaty TD Walter L. Cole called for a major investment in public housing. He described the tenements as a 'national scandal' demanding that

> at the earliest possible moment we should clear them out and erase them from the face of the earth; and if we do not do so we deserve to be held in contempt by any people priding themselves on their civilisation.[19]

His call went unheeded as the rural bias in housing policy continued. The same year saw the passing of the 1923 Land Act granting compulsory purchase powers to Councils to acquire and sell on land. The Act marked the end of a lengthy period of land reform and redistribution and benefited a further 114,000 tenants.

Increased grants and rates relief were provided to those seeking to build private homes in the Housing Act of 1924 giving particular priority to those building larger houses. These supports were extended to building cooperatives known as Public Utility Societies the following year.

Further assistance was made available in a third Housing Act in 1929 through the extension of a Central Government loan fund to provide mortgages under the Small Dwellings Acquisitions scheme while rates relief was made mandatory for all new homeowners.

The 1926 census estimated that there were as many as 800,000 people living in overcrowded accommodation. As a result, infant mortality in working-class neighbourhoods was three times that in middle-class areas and 4,500 people were losing their lives to TB every year.[20] The Department of Local Government estimated that the State needed 43,656 homes, yet despite the various initiatives output remained low.

The combined consequence of these measures over the decade was a total public investment of £2.58 million in house construction of which £1.07 million went to private individuals. By 1932 Local Authorities had provided an additional 10,000 homes while private builders had delivered 16,500. In Dublin City, where need for Council housing was highest, the Local Authority provided a meagre 483 units a year over the decade. According to O'Connell, 'two thirds of all houses built with State aid were in private ownership'.[21]

However, as with the housing funded under the million pound scheme, both the rural and urban housing funded through the various housing acts of the 1920s benefited small farmers and the artisan working class. The State's first Taoiseach, W.T. Cosgrave, made clear that Government had no intention of seeking to address the housing problems of the poorest in society. He told a Dáil debate in 1925 that doing so would require the provision of 70,000 homes at a cost of £14 million. A cost he clearly felt was prohibitive.[22]

Despite the fact that tens of thousands of families continued to live in the most appalling conditions in the cities and towns it would not be until the 1930s that social action and civic concern would force the political system to act.

The 1920s did, however, generate one of the first sustained debates about the issue of town planning and whether the solution to the poor housing conditions in the urban centres lay in the building of new suburbs. Civic surveys for Cork and Dublin were published in 1922 and 1923. The Dublin report described the housing situation is Dublin as a 'tragedy', stating:

> Its conditions cause either a rapid or slow death. Rapid when the houses fall upon the tenants, as has already happened, slow when they remain standing dens of insanitation.[23]

The survey warned that the tenements were at risk of spreading and urged the rehousing of 60,000 people to new housing developments in the suburbs. O'Connell notes that the survey's findings were strongly supported by the officials in Dublin Corporation but that political support was less than forthcoming.

Cumann an nGaedhael TD John Good summed up the thinking of Government at the time when he argued that

> housing is an economic problem which could only be solved by putting it on an economic basis ... we must learn in the Free State to rely more on ourselves and less on the Government and to try and earn what we want by honest work.[24]

In what was to become an almost universal myopia in successive Government thinking, exchequer subsidies were acceptable and supplied in great volume where housing was to be provided for private ownership but the call for similar subsidies to lift society's poorest families from the most appalling living conditions was seemingly unthinkable. O'Connell concludes that

> the thrust of housing legislation throughout the 1920's had only a marginal effect on alleviating the dire living conditions of the poorest urban households. The greatest benefits accrued to the middle class and better off working class households whose incomes allowed them to avail of the subsidies contained in the various housing acts of the new Irish state.[25]

This was a far cry from the founding policy document of the Irish Republic, the 1919 Democratic Programme. One of the very first acts of the newly established First Dáil was to assert that it shall

> be the first duty of the Government of the Republic to make provisions for the physical, mental and spiritual well-being of the children to ensure that no child shall

suffer hunger or cold from lack of food, clothing or shelter ...[26]

The gap between the rhetoric and reality of the new Republic was to become the key battle ground in the general election that brought Cumann an nGaedhael's first decade in power to an end in 1931. It would also be the measure against which working-class communities and their trade union and political representatives would judge the new Fianna Fáil Government of Éamon de Valera.

New Government, Similar Policy

The final years of W.T. Cosgrave's Government were marked by growing social unrest, in part fuelled by the failure of his administration to address the social and economic needs of large sections of society. Fianna Fáil's entry to Government in 1931, assisted by a more assertive Labour Party and grass roots campaigning by radical republicans, was as much on a promise of addressing the issues of unemployment and poor housing as it was on broader constitutional issues such as partition. Indeed, leading radicals within the party such as Constance Markievicz urged their colleagues to ensure that politics 'was more about the organisation of food, clothing and housing' than which leader to mobilise under.[27]

While the final Housing Act of Cumann na nGaedhael in 1931, provoked by a particularly damning Dublin Corporation Housing report of the same year, finally opened the way for subsidies to provide housing for lower-income families, it was the first housing act of the new Fianna Fáil Government that made such developments genuinely viable.

The 1932 Act provided additional funds to Local Authorities to offset the loan costs of rehousing those cleared from slums or for lower-income urban or rural workers. The new facility meant that rents could be sent at a less than economic cost enabling lower-income families access to housing.

The legislation still prioritised development by private individuals and Public Utility Societies and as with its predecessors was more focused on rural labourers than their urban counterparts. Over the following eight years 17,525 cottages were provided for rural labourers, despite only 10,000 being required. Meanwhile less than half the 19,000 urban dwellings required in Dublin were built.[28] In total 99,000 homes were provided under the terms of the act with 56,000 in private ownership.[29]

The increasing reliance on private loan finance started to encounter problems as Irish banks, operating as a cartel, increasingly set prohibitive interest rates. In response Government expanded the availability of their Local Loans Fund to cover housing, though neither Cork nor Dublin cities were eligible despite having the greatest need.

One of the immediate consequences of the freeing up of credit was to see the number of Small Dwelling Acquisitions Scheme builds and purchases dramatically increase. In the scheme's first four decades 2,102 mortgages were issued. In the following decade 4,648 homes were purchased with the loan.

While Fianna Fáil made much of what they called their 'Housing Drive' others were less than convinced. Housing activism, led by the Republic Congress, the Communist Party and others gathered pace throughout the 1930s. A series of proposed evictions for rent arrears in Council housing in Dublin provoked widespread anger and the formation of the Municipal Tenants Association. Rent arrears and consequent rent strikes once again highlighted the problem that economic rents, set to allow Local Authorities to repay their loans, were too high for low-income families, especially when faced with economic downturns.

There was also growing disquiet at the emerging relationship between building contractors and the new Fianna Fáil Government. J.J. Lee notes that

> The housing programme naturally provided grist to the pockets of the contractors. Fortunes were made in the field more easily than manufacturing. The building industry soon came to be widely regarded as an extension of the Fianna Fáil patronage system.[30]

Though Lee did acknowledge that, irrespective of the motivations behind the building expansion, 'the new dwellings were a marked improvement on the foul slums that for so long had disgraced Dublin and other cities'.[31]

Notwithstanding these concerns, output of Government-funded housing significantly increased during the 1930s. In the decade from 1932 an average of 12,000 houses were built annually of which half were Council homes, compared to an average of just 2,000 per year under the previous administration. However, from the early 1940s this dropped off significantly as fiscal constraints and the disruption to the supply of building materials caused by the Second World War impacted on house building.

Nevertheless, even with the increased output the new Government's policy was remarkably similar to their predecessor's. Private homeownership was prioritised over public housing while the latter predominantly favoured better-off workers and the middle class.

While in part this reflected the financial constraints of the time, it was also based on a deep-seated prejudice towards those trapped in poverty.

During a revealing debate on slum clearance in 1931 the then Minister for Supplies Seán Lemass told the Dáil that

> The ratepayer who has to pay for slum clearance and re-housing is sceptical of the use of helping the slum dweller ... [they] will tell you that money spent on slum clearance and re-housing the slum dweller is largely wasted.

Lemass went on to argue that the best way to 'counteract that argument' is to 'show that a person who has lived all his life in the slums is capable of being taught how to care for property'. The future Taoiseach urged the use of 'instructors and other people capable of educating and training' slum dwellers when they move into new homes, a practice apparently used in 'certain English cities'. Though Lemass wondered 'whether that system would be suitable to the Irish character'.[32]

However, Lemass, better than most, fully understood the need for Fianna Fáil to drive a wedge between urban working-class voters and both the Labour Party and more radical social activism. Thus while their housing policy didn't depart in substance from their predecessor's, its quantity was certainly higher as evidenced by the increase in social spending from £8 million in 1929 to £12.6 million by 1939.[33]

In what was to become a regular feature of all subsequent Governments, significant disagreements emerged during the 1930s between the Minister and Department for Finance on the one hand and high-spending Departments such as Local Government on the other. While de Valera erred on the side of electoral caution during the 1930s the balance started to swing in Finance's direction in the following decade.

But like Cumann na nGaedhael before them much of the focus remained on private ownership. Within a year of taking office Fianna Fáil almost doubled the subsidy for cottage building to 60 percent of the value of the Council loan repayments.[34]

The 1930s also saw the emergence of questionable building practices as Local Authorities, under pressure to deliver new homes, reduced standards in a practice known at the time as 'skinning down'. The 1932 legislation provided subsidies to the Councils on a per unit basis creating a perverse incentive to produce a greater number of units at a lower cost.

The consequences were soon felt by tenants who discovered that their new homes were not built to an adequate standard. The longer-term legacy for Councils were only to be discovered when future generations had to bear the cost of substantial regeneration. Despite strong criticism at the time from the Dublin City Housing Architect, the practice was widespread.

While such 'innovations' were clearly not welcome developments, other more positive policy ideas did emerge during the 1930s. In response to the problem of whether to charge lower-income tenants economic rents or affordable rents the manager of Cork City Council Philip Monaghan introduced a system of rents as a percentage of family income. What became known as differential rent was eventually applied across all Local Authorities and remains in place today.

Despite the increased output, need, particularly in cities and towns, remained high. The Emergency brought new construction to dangerously low levels. The Dublin Housing Inquiry published in 1943 estimated that an additional 43,000 new dwellings were needed to replace the tenements in Dublin, Cork, Limerick and Waterford.

However, unlike the post-war Government in Westminster and its ambitious plans for substantial public investment in health and housing under the socialist Minister Aneurin Bevan, there was no post-war optimism in evidence in the Fianna Fáil Minister for Local Government Seán MacEntee.

Indeed, as need continued to increase output continued to decline, reaching an all-time low in 1946 when just 563 houses were built.

Fianna Fáil's failure to tackle the urban housing crisis was one of the key reasons for its fall from office. The emerging electoral threat of the new left republican party Clann na Poblachta was grounded in a growing disenchantment at the failure of the Free State after twenty-five years to improve the standard of living of a significant number of the urban and rural working class.

A Reforming Coalition

Despite his attempt to thwart the rise of Clann na Poblachta by calling a snap election in February 1948 Éamon de Valera was unable to stop the formation of the Free State's first coalition Government, bringing his seventeen-year run as Taoiseach to an end. The new Government was an incongruous collection of Fine Gael, two Labour parties, Clann na Poblachta and a small farmers' party.

However, despite its eclectic nature it had a reforming zeal which brought some of the post-war State interventionism gathering pace in Britain and Europe to bear on areas of policy including health and housing.

In housing this was led by Labour Minister Timothy Murphy until his unexpected death in 1949; he was then replaced by his party colleague Michael Keyes. Murphy not only significantly increased the targets for housing output for the coming years but exerted significant pressure on the banks to increase lending into the construction sector and delivered a tenfold increase in output within four years.[35] He was also assisted by the availability of funding from the Marshall Aid Programme.

The 1946 census reported that there were 310,265 houses without any sanitation and 80,000 people were still living in single-room dwellings with 23,000 in Dublin.[36]

The first significant development on the housing front was the 1948 White Paper which reviewed policy to date and attempted to set out a longer-term plan to deal with both current and future demand. Important considerations such a migration, population change, property obsolescence, overcrowding and the need to raise accommodation standards were central to its considerations.

The White Paper estimated that the State needed 100,000 new homes over the next decade and argued that 60 percent of these should be public. To achieve this ambitious target the report recommended a range of changes to the existing regime of subsidies including halving the interest rate of the Local Loans Fund, extending the repaying period from 25 to 50 years and the provision of lump sum grants to Councils.

The subsequent 1948 Housing Act also increased the maximum market value of houses to be purchased under the Small Dwellings Scheme, increased home buyer grants and introduced a new supplementary grant for lower-income home buyers.

The results of these measures were significant with both social and private housing output increasing over the following ten years. Keogh notes that 'in a spirit of new age optimism' Government's capital expenditure increased to £120 million including £6 million of borrowing the bulk of which was to fund houses and hospitals.[37] Social housing output doubled from the 1940s to the 1950s from 20,768 houses in the first decade to 52,500 in the second while private output increased from 37,164 during the 40s to 49,188 in the 50s.[38]

While housing output increased significantly, the ratio of social to private housing shifted dramatically in favour of the latter from the early 1960s with just 29,124 social units delivered in that decade compared with 64,835 private homes. Kenna confirms that despite the significant increase in Council house provision, Government subsidies still benefited the private home buyer more than the social renting tenant:

> In the 16 years from April 1948, about 137,000 dwellings were built with State aid, of which 74,000 were provided by private enterprise and 63,000 by local authorities. Capital expenditure in the period 1948 to 1964 on housing was estimated at £225m. Of which State aid and local authorities contributed £192m.[39]

Significantly just 15 percent of total capital invested in housing during this period came from non-State sources demonstrating the extent to which the vast majority of housing, including private homeownership, relied on non-market sources for funding.

Michelle Norris notes that the 'take-up of central government house purchase and reconstruction grants increased from 2,157 in 1948/1949 to 17,544 in 1963/1964. This reflects the fact that, contrary to the 1948 White Paper's expectations, '70% of dwellings constructed during the 1960s were provided by the private sector primarily for owner-occupation.'[40]

The short-lived 14th Dáil brought Fianna Fáil back to power for three years during which investment in and output of housing was scaled back by the fiscally orthodox Minister Seán McEntee and his officials at the Department of Finance.

However, with the return of the coalition Government in 1954 the expansion of house building was resumed well into the 1960s. As increased supply addressed much of the acute housing need, it also led to renewed concerns about the absence of adequate planning as new estates provided homes but not necessarily with the necessary social and economic infrastructure to meet the needs of communities. Concerns also continued regarding the growing economic and political significance of the construction industry and its relationship to Fianna Fáil who were back in Government from 1957 for a straight eleven-year run.

As the 1950s were coming to a close a new source of opposition to continued expenditure on housing emerged. Thomas Whitaker's 1958 First Programme for Economic Expansion argued strongly for a shift in public expenditure from social to productive sectors of the economy.[41] Housing constituted the single largest area of social expenditure through capital funds, loans and tax reliefs. While little understood at the time, this prioritising of 'productive' over 'social' investment and the negative social costs that come with it, was to have a profound impact on Government thinking for decades to come.

In 1962 Dublin Corporation has almost 9,000 households on their waiting lists with almost half of these deemed to have an immediate need. In the same year just 1,035 new council homes were under construction.[42]

While house building continued to increase, slum conditions remained a reality for many as highlighted by the death of four people including two children in 1963 when two tenement buildings collapsed within a fortnight in June, first in Bolton Street and then Fenian Street, only a short walk from Dáil Éireann and Government Buildings. The Dublin Housing Action Campaign was formed in response to the tragedy demanding the demolition of the tenements and the provision of safe and adequate housing.

A second Housing White Paper was published in 1964 and estimated that 50,000 new homes were needed immediately to meet existing demand. The paper also projected a need for a further 98,000 homes up to 1970, 50 percent of which were to be provided by Local Authorities. This would require the largest output of housing in the history of the State at 14,000 units per year.

In the same year officials and elected members from Dublin Corporation visited Paris, Copenhagen and Stockholm to examine how new building technologies, including system built concrete apartments, could be used to meet housing need at home. The trip was important as it not only secured a commitment to deliver an additional 1,000 homes a year over the next three years but was also seminal in the future use of high-rise housing developments.[43]

The 1964 White Paper was quickly followed by the 1966 Housing Act which consolidated all of the existing housing legislation of the preceding half a century into a single piece of law. In addition to providing further incentives to private homeownership, including the provision of low-cost sites for self-builders, it also extended the right of purchase to all Local Authority tenants. The results were quite dramatic.

Despite only becoming available in the second half of the decade Local Authorities sold 64,490 Council homes by 1969, more than double the output of social homes in the same decade. Significant discounts of up to 30 percent for urban purchasers and 45 percent for rural purchasers were available, determined by the length of time in the tenancy.

In response to demands for a more planned approach to housing output the Government introduced a requirement on Councils to produce development plans via the Local Government (Planning and Development) Act 1963. Combined with the 1968 Buchanan Report new suburban population centres in Tallaght, Clondalkin, Lucan and Blanchardstown were proposed. Forty years after it was first suggested, suburbanisation was to become official Government policy.

This newfound optimism was evident in the zeal with which the Minister for the Environment Neil Blaney belatedly embraced the post-war ambition of his British counterparts. A new National Building Agency with significant funds at its disposal was set to work with Local Authorities to deliver the largest scale housing projects in the history of the State, best exemplified by the proposed 3,000-home development in Ballymun at a cost of more than £9 million and the 1,000-home suburban development in Moy Ross in Limerick.

But Government hubris – as evidenced in the naming of the Ballymun towers after the signatories of the 1916 Proclamation – was not matched by long-term investment. The peripheral location of the larger developments combined with lack of amenities and poor allocation and estate management policies were to turn these iconic projects of the late 1960s into notorious examples of poor housing policy by the 1990s.

Social Housing's High Point

The 1970s witnessed the largest output of housing in the history of the State with 61,953 social and 176,230 private homes built. However, with the massive transfer of stock from the public to the private sector via tenant purchase the overall balance in favour of homeownership continued to prevail.

Private homeownership increased dramatically between 1946 and 1971 from 52.6 percent to 70 percent statewide and from 26 percent to 48 percent in Dublin and 13 percent to 49 percent in Cork. Nevertheless, significant social housing output also saw Council housing as a percentage of the overall housing stock during this period increase from 16.5 percent to 18.4 percent.

The late 60s and early 70s was also a period of increasing investment in city centre commercial development with significant private and semi-State developments replacing some of the historic core of Dublin City. As slums were cleared, speculative developers could make significant gains replacing Georgian terraces with modern office blocks. The result was a profound change to the streetscape and aesthetics of large parts of the city centre generating strong opposition from the Georgian Society, high profile cultural figures and members of the public. That the Fianna Fáil Minister for Local Government unsurprisingly took the side of 'progress' – and the developer – dismissing the protestors as 'belted earls', was a sign of the increasing political strength of those who had money to invest in property.[44]

The significant increase in private housing output brought a new dynamic into play, namely land price inflation. As residential development increasingly took place in suburbs, once-agricultural land would significantly rise in price when zoned for residential use. Of course, the increase in value had nothing to do with the land itself or the efforts of the owners, but was a direct result of both the decision to rezone and the provision of infrastructure such as roads and services by the Local Authorities.

In one example, serviced land in County Dublin rose in price in a single year from £1,100 per acre to £7,000 – a 536 percent increase in value.

In response the Government commissioned respected judge John Kenny to examine the issue of land management and bring forward recommendations to curb the ever escalating cost of land. The 1972 *Report from the Committee on the Price of Land* made a series of radical proposals which have been quoted as often as they have been ignored.

Amongst the options considered were price controls, development levies, direct payment to Local Authorities for services, various tax measures and nationalisation. The report stated a clear preference for the compulsory purchase of private land in high demand areas at original use value plus 25 percent of the uplift expected from residential zoning.

The land could then either be used for social housing or sold on to developers at below market prices for private development.

The recommendations of the report were never implemented. Land price inflation, and with it house price inflation, remained a significant problem in the housing system. Subsequent generations of policy-makers would return time and again to the same debate as a housing boom would re-present the very same problems as those which the Fianna Fail Government of the late 1960s and Fine Gael–Labour Government of the early 1970s failed to address.

While social housing output expanded significantly during the 1970s private ownership raced ahead. The decade saw private sector building increase threefold, and Government placed ever greater emphasis on subsidising private homeownership through grants and tenant purchase. A further 59,566 Council homes were sold at significant discounts to tenants in that decade, almost the same number as new Council homes built by Local Authorities.

Housing in the 1970s, a White Paper published in 1969, once again emphasised the State's preference for owner-occupation on both social and economic grounds. According to Kenna, a National Economic and Social Council research paper published later in the decade confirmed that 'in 1975, the aggregate proportionate subsidisation of owner-occupiers was greater than that of local authority tenants'.[45]

In the same year social housing hit what was to be its highest ever level of output at 8,800. Never again was the State to produce as many Council homes in a single year. Indeed, through the 1970s and early 80s social housing output never fell below 20 percent of total housing output with the single exception of 1981.

Finally, after half a century the Southern State was finally getting to grips with current housing need and providing a sufficient supply of both private and public homes to meet the vast majority of demand. The slums had been cleared, waiting lists were small and short. Norris described this period as 'the saturation phase', as during this period, the land project was extended to its furthest practicable limits and public subsidisation of homeownership was extended from the rural population to the urban middle class (via subsidies such as grants and rates remission and local government loans) and also to the working class in the cities (via the extension of tenant purchase of social housing.[46]

While there is no doubt that between the end of the Emergency and the early 1970s the housing need of ever growing sections of Irish society was being met, including that of lower-income families, other groups in society continued to be left behind.

Government policy and legislation was still blind to those with no homes at all. As a result, students in Trinity College Dublin founded the first Irish branch of the Simon Communities in 1969. Inspired by the pioneering work of Anton Wallich-Clifford, who founded the Simon Communities in London in 1963, the group aimed to highlight the plight of rough sleepers and those without any accommodation and to provide on a voluntary basis some form of emergency accommodation.

The other group who remained invisible to official Ireland was the Travelling Community. While the *Report of the Commission on Itinerancy* in 1963 brought the issue of Travellers into the mainstream of policy debate it did so by seeking to eradicate the nomadic culture of Travellers by forcing them into settled housing. The move failed and simply forced Travellers into illegal occupation of roadside camps.

It would take several decades before Government policy and legislation even started to grapple with the issues of homelessness and Traveller-appropriate accommodation in any serious way.

As is so often the case public opinion was more alert to the contradictions evident in the proximity of continued acute housing need with a construction boom and dramatically rising land values. Alongside radical left republican campaigns for better housing were increasingly vocal social justice advocates from within the faith communities. Logos, a left-wing catholic group active on housing issues, was founded by John Feeney. A Dominican priest, Fr Ferghal O'Connor, founded Ally, a housing charity for single parents.

Priests were also using their influence in broadcasting to highlight housing inequalities much to the ire of the Government. A 1968 broadcast of the RTÉ show *Outlook* edited by Fr Austin Flannery, featured a discussion on the housing issue with the Jesuit Michael Sweetman and Communist Party of Ireland spokesperson Michael O'Riordan. The Minister for Local Government accused Flannery of an 'abuse of privilege' by a 'so called cleric' while the Minister for Finance and future Taoiseach Charles Haughey dismissed the priest as 'gullible'. The very public spat continued into the pages of the week's newspapers with a formal rebuttal from Flannery in the *Evening Herald*. For his efforts in highlighting the plight of those not served by Government housing policy the Garda Special Branch allocated an officer to sit in studio for every future Flannery-produced show.[47]

Conclusion

The politics of housing provision from 1870 to the early 1970s displays a number of dynamics that shaped and continues to shape the Irish housing system into the twenty-first century.

There is a cycle that starts with intolerable conditions: urban and rural poverty, insecurity of tenure, high rents and illegal evictions. The everyday inequality and unfairness of the housing system reaches some tipping point in the form of famine, disease or building collapse, all of which involve death.

Frustration and anger turn to social mobilisation whether through the Land League, trade union movement or Housing Action Committees. People at the sharp edge of a bad, abnormal, difficult, dysfunctional housing system mobilise in their tens of thousands in rural Ireland and their thousands in the cities and towns.

In turn politicians, both honest and expedient, take notice and join the fray, passing motions and lobbying for legislative change. Under pressure in parliament and facing the very real potential for social revolt and the collapse of public order Government responds in a slow and piecemeal fashion.

The pace of reform is determined by the strength of the social mobilisation and the coherence of the organisations through which those most affected organise their efforts.

Progress in land reform and rural housing at the turn of the century far outstripped change in urban Ireland because the size and strength of the land movement was so much greater than their urban counterparts.

However, what is more striking than the disparity between urban and rural housing policy during the first half of the twentieth century is the underlying principle guiding both, namely promoting owner-occupation.

Almost all of the legislative and policy responses to housing need, first by Westminster and then the Free State Government, were based on a single principle, private ownership. Land purchase, rural cottages and even some urban charitable and public housing would be owned by the tenants purchased through low interest, long-term loans.

It is remarkable that by 1914 Government had provided 45,000 homes, 82 percent in rural areas, through various loan schemes. In Britain, the Government had built a mere 24,000. But whereas in twentieth-century Britain public housing would predominantly be Council owned, in Ireland the State was less eager to take up the role of landlord. Rather it saw its function as assisting working people, both rural and urban, is accessing credit to own their own homes.

While funding for the provision of subsidised housing for the very poor would start to emerge before partition, in reality it was not until 1932 that public housing delivered by Local Authorities would become a significant feature of the housing system.

Even here, the dramatic expansion of tenant purchase from the 1960s meant that public housing would become a significant gateway to private homeownership for tens of thousands of families.

Private homeownership for the majority with a small supply of public housing for the very poor was to become the policy framework in which successive Governments in Dublin responded to housing need.

Michelle Norris, in her ground-breaking study *Property, Family and the Irish Welfare State* characterises the dramatic scale of State intervention in private homeownership as 'asset based welfare'. She challenges the argument that the Southern Irish State, in contrast to many of its liberal and social democratic neighbours, failed to develop a comprehensive welfare regime.

Instead she contends that, rather than developing a welfare state that focuses on the redistribution of income and provision of social services that was the hallmark of the welfare regimes elsewhere, Irish Governments prioritised ownership of property.

Thus rather than a welfare state based on a grand bargain between workers and employers, a distinctively Irish system emerged from the grand bargain between landlords and tenant farmers underpinned by low interest, long-term subsidised loans for the purchase of land and housing.

Publicly owned housing was and would always remain peripheral to this system as Governments were slowly dragged into meeting the housing needs of the urban working class and rural landless labourers.

As housing policy developed throughout the first half of the twentieth century other key issues did emerge including planning, land management and value, and the relationship between industry and politicians. While each of these was to become more important from the 1970s onwards they remained peripheral to the key issue of ownership.

By the 1970s those issues that had dominated housing insecurity for the majority only decades earlier – illegal eviction, rack renting, tenement slums – were now thankfully a thing of the past. But not for everyone.

The dramatic rise in owner-occupation and the provision of public housing meant that 87 percent of people had a secure home. But for the 13 percent remaining in an unregulated private rental sector or left to fend for themselves on the roadside in illegal halting sites not much had changed since partition.

And even for those with secure homes, poor quality construction during the 1930s meant many, particularly in older public housing, could rightly complain of poor conditions. The failure of Government to ensure that

Local Councils had sufficient funds to maintain their stock of social housing to adequate standards would remain a serious issue into the future.

The late 1970s was certainly the high point in housing provision of the twentieth century. That decade marked the apex of the State's involvement in the direct funding and provision of housing whether for owner-occupiers or social rental tenants.

But there were also problems. State intervention wasn't consistent enough, as each time Government appeared to be getting on top of housing need they would take their foot off the pedal and reduce expenditure. Not all slums were cleared and not all housing was of a good standard. And beneath the surface of the system lay significant vulnerabilities, kept out of sight by massive levels of State subsidies whether in the form of grants, loans or tax breaks.

In the following decades the structure of our dysfunctional system did not change much but the financing of it did. These changes, detailed in the next chapter, revealed the weaknesses within the system as it had been designed to date while at the same time introducing new risks and vulnerabilities which in turn would generate levels of housing insecurity and need that many thought were now a thing of the past.

Movement 2

The State Walks Away

Recession and Retrenchment

If the 1970s can be characterised as the high point of direct State intervention in the financing and provision of housing, then the 1980s marks both a turning point and significant decline. While this change did not affect the shape of our dysfunctional housing system it dramatically altered the way in which that system is financed. This in turn exposed the vulnerabilities of the existing system while simultaneously introducing new risks.

Underpinning the significant expansion of public investment in social housing and supports for owner-occupation in the 1960s and 1970s was a period of sustained economic growth. While this continued into the early 1980s, the onset of recession as the decade progressed was to provide part of the impetus of the withdrawal of the State from direct expenditure on housing.

This fiscal crisis of State gathered pace from the end of the 1970s and affected economies at both the core and the periphery of the developed world as post-war Keynesianism came up against economic stagnation, rising prices and wage demands. The stage was set for a major ideological reformation in the advanced economies as the social democratic compromise that prevailed since 1945 gave way to renewed liberalisation.

The elections of Margaret Thatcher in 1979 and Ronald Reagan in 1981 signalled a shift in economic policy that would engulf most overdeveloped countries for the coming decades. The consequence was increased financial liberalisation coupled with reduced taxes, particularly on wealth, combined with reductions in social expenditure. The era of neoliberalism was born.

The impact on housing policy, in Ireland as elsewhere, was dramatic as a confluence of interests coincided, with profound consequences for the financing and in turn the availability of accommodation.

Concerns with the increasing cost of subsidies for private home purchase were already emerging in Southern Ireland during the latter part of the 1970s. Norris notes repeated breaches by Councils of the Local Loans Fund lending limits, due to the popularity of the scheme. There was a genuine fear in some quarters that this could lead to a significant funding crisis in the Local Government sector and so a number of changes were made.[1]

Limits were placed on the total value of Mortgage Interest Tax Relief that buyers could claim in 1974. Home purchase grants were restricted to first-time buyers for the first time in 1977. And the complex array of supports for would-be owner-occupiers were replaced by a single grant. Meanwhile Government simultaneously sought to encourage greater Building Society lending to offset the restrictions in direct State subsidies.[2]

However, during the 1980s as the recession took hold the economic situation deteriorated significantly. By 1987 unemployment was at 17 percent, Government debt stood at 150 percent of GDP and servicing this debt was absorbing 27 percent of public expenditure.

The Government response was threefold: a dramatic reduction in capital expenditure on social housing, a similar reduction in supports for private home purchasers, and a liberalisation of building society and bank lending. The impacts of these changes and a number of associated supplementary interventions were profound.

Reduction and Residualisation

The 1980s witnessed a 30 percent drop in the output of social housing with 42,893 homes delivered in that decade compared to 61,953 during the 1970s.[3] However, these figures hide the more dramatic impact of the spending cuts from 1987 onwards. In 1984 Government funded 7,007 social homes. In the following years it fell significantly, to 6,523 units in 1985, 5,517 in 1986, 3,200 in 1987 and 1,450 units in 1988. It hit a historic low in 1989 with just 768 homes.[4] It would be almost two decades before output would recover to the average levels of the late 1970s and early 1980s.

While the reduced expenditure may have eased the pressure on the Department of Finance it had the opposite effect on levels of housing need. In response Government sought to leverage existing stock to offset these losses and free up houses or funds.

The 1984 Surrender Grant of £5,000 introduced by Fine Gael was an attempt to meet two policy objectives with a single measure. Higher earning Council tenants, armed with a substantial taxpayer funded grant, could move out of their Council estate and purchase a newly built home on a private estate, thus fulfilling the Government's housing policy priority of encouraging homeownership and promoting new construction. Meanwhile much-needed

Council homes would be freed up for those on the waiting lists.

In the four years the scheme was under operation, up to 8,000 Council properties were surrendered, equal to almost half the total output of new Council homes during the same period.[5] The surrenders were heavily concentrated in a small number of estates with 75 percent of the Dublin properties located in just four areas, Darndale, Ballymun, Clondalkin and Tallaght.[6] All of those households availing of the grant were in employment.

While it is important not to overstate the significance of the grant given the relatively small numbers involved (approximately 6 percent of total social housing stock), the concentration in certain estates and its short life span, the impact was nonetheless significant.

Firstly, it reduced considerably the income mix in the estates affected, many of which already had high concentrations of poverty and social welfare dependence. The arrival of heroin in many of those areas from the early 1980s and the accompanying sensationalist media stories of 'problem estates' riven with drugs and crime combined to create a public perception of Council estates as ghettos and social housing as bad housing.

It also marked a shift in Government thinking and practice with respect to who Council housing was for. A report by Threshold, the country's leading charity supporting renters, in 1987 described the Surrender Grant as having the effect of 'concentrating disadvantage' in certain areas. Their study highlighted the fact that allocation practices in many Councils shifted considerably during this period with a greater number of single-parent families and people transitioning from homelessness securing allocations by the end of the surrender grants operation.[7]

Tenant purchase was also initially affected by the onset of the recession with a significant fall off in the number of Council homes bought annually from 1983. While purchases had averaged at 4,000 units a year for most of the previous decade 1983 saw a decline starting at 3,492 purchases in that year dropping to a low of 533 in 1986.[8] While a recovery of sorts took place in the following two years Government responded with a new heavily discounted scheme in 1988.[9] The response was dramatic, with purchases jumping to 18,166 in 1989, the highest on record.

The consequence of these measures, particularly as they continued into the 1990s, was to significantly alter both the perception and the reality of social housing. Norris is correct when she argues that

> No matter what the intent of the reforms of the 1980s, their effect was to redefine the role of social housing: it ceased to become available to workers on low incomes and instead became welfare housing, increasingly targeted on a narrow range of long term welfare dependent households. The association between poverty and social housing tenure had always been present to some degree ... But from the mid 1980s, the association of social housing with poverty became more direct.[10]

However, it is important to stress that as tenant purchasers remained in their existing estates the actual impact of the policy changes of the 1980s had a greater impact on future social housing developments and allocations. As tenant purchasers were generally the higher earning tenants, Councils also lost a significant portion of their rental revenue, impacting on their ability to maintain the remaining stock.

The End of Asset-Based Welfare

While the level of State support for private home buyers had started to reduce during the 1970s its role was still significant. In 1966/67 Small Dwelling Acquisition loans accounted for 32 percent of all mortgage lending. By 1972/73 it had fallen but still covered 18 percent of new loans.[11] Despite the placing of a ceiling on the total value of Mortgage Interest Tax Relief in 1974, it still covered 23 percent of the total price of the purchase of the home for mortgages taken out in 1975.[12]

However, throughout the 1980s private purchaser supports were increasingly restricted. In 1982 the £3,000 grant for first-time buyers was extended to five years. In 1986 it was replaced with a smaller £2,250 builders grant for first-time buyers of new buildings only. Existing home improvement grants were abolished the following year. In 1988 the income limit for Small Dwelling Acquisition loans was further reduced and for the first time limited to those unable to secure loans from commercial lenders.[13] The decade ended with a further reduction in the Mortgage Interest Tax Relief ceiling.

Taken together the changes to supports for both social housing and subsidised owner-occupation saw a 60 percent reduction in expenditure on housing as a percentage of GDP from 1975 to 1990. Nevertheless, working families who wanted to own their own homes had an alternative source of finance, namely the banks and building societies, which in the short term at least would ensure than unlike those dependent on social housing, private homeowners could have a non-state source of finance to ensure access to a home.

Letting Private Finance In

Ending direct subsidies and tax relief for would-be homeowners was more a fiscal necessity than an ideological preference for both the Fine Gael and Fianna Fáil Governments of the 1980s. However, it could not be allowed to undermine both parties' core policy objective, namely homeownership. Thus while the liberalisation of bank lending would be a key ideological plank of both the Reagan and Thatcher regimes, Ireland was an early convert and for much more practical reasons.

Pádraig Flynn, the then Fianna Fáil Minister for Environment, made clear the logic of his support for bank liberalisation in 1987 when he claimed that despite reductions in Government loans for home purchase, private finance would provide 'an adequate supply of mortgages for all income groups in all areas'.[14]

While the primary driver of the restrictions to and reductions in direct Government loans for home buyers was to cut expenditure, it was also designed to ensure that the 'competitive advantage' held by the Local Government sector was removed to 'encourage' greater lending by banks and building societies.

In an attempt to boost the volume of Building Society mortgages the Government introduced a short-term subsidy to bring down interest rates in 1981 and increased the subsidy again in 1982. However, take up of loans from this sector remained sluggish, in part because of the requirement for many borrowers to have deposits ranging from 20 percent to 30 percent. In response, and in an attempt to get banks directly involved in lending, the preferential treatment for Building Societies was ended in 1983 and Central Bank credit rules were replaced with indicative guidelines the following year.[15]

Further financial reforms were introduced restricting price setting by banks, facilitating Building Society lending for bridging and refurbishment loans and allowing societies access to inter-bank lending. By the end of the decade Government policy was firmly focused on ensuring private finance was the principal provider of mortgage lending into the future.[16]

Despite the significant withdrawal of traditional State support for home purchasers, the number of new mortgages increased from 27,632 in 1986 to 38,580 in 1989 providing the Government with comfort that their shift from public to private finance for owner-occupiers was working.[17]

The shift was in line with developments elsewhere in the Anglo-Saxon world. For much of the twentieth century, mortgage lending in Britain was the preserve of Building Societies. However, in response to bank liberalisation in the United States, Margaret Thatcher introduced significant changes in both 1979 and 1986, opening the United Kingdom market to greater foreign competition and inter-bank lending.

Building Societies were also allowed access to the wholesale markets, further increasing the volume of credit available to the British mortgage market. Not only did borrowing for home purchase increase but a new phenomenon of equity withdrawal (borrowing against the value of your home) became an increasingly popular means for households financing other areas of expenditure.

The result according to Josh Ryan-Collins was a dramatic increase in the volume of mortgage-related lending, which jumped from 20 percent of Gross Domestic Product in the late 1970s to 55 percent a decade later.[18] The immediate impact of this financial deregulation was the British housing bubble of the 1980s, which was to cause significant problems when it burst in the 1990s. Nevertheless, much less obvious at the time was the impact of credit liberalisation on house prices.

Ryan-Collins argues in his recent book *Why Can't You Afford a Home?* that the most significant impact was a dramatic increase in house prices as mortgage finance actively sought out ever increasing house and land price values which were not only more profitable than standard investment in the productive economy but also more secure. He argues that up to the 1960s house prices were relatively stable irrespective of changes in income and population. However, from the 1960s to the 1990s house prices jumped by a dramatic 65 percent.[19] His conclusion is that the 'evidence suggests that the Anglo-Saxon economies that deregulated their mortgage markets in the 1980s saw faster rises and more volatility than those economies that did not'.[20]

While the impact of credit liberalisation on house prices in Southern Ireland was more delayed than in Britain, it did eventually arrive, albeit assisted by a second wave of financial deregulation led by the European Union in the 1990s and access to cheap credit arising from membership of the single currency.

By the end of the 1980s, however, the more significant outcome was a successful transition from a State funded property-owning housing system to a private finance-led model. In 1971, 68 percent of homes were owner-occupied, the figure rose to 74 percent in 1981 and higher still to 79 percent in 1991.

When taken together, the reductions in public expenditure on social housing and private buyer subsidies coupled with the liberalisation of mortgage finance brought about the end of the State's role as the principal funder and provider of housing. The era of asset-based welfare that had been in place for more than half a century was coming to a close. While social and owner-occupier supports would continue in the future, they would be much more peripheral to both Government policy and the overall operation of the housing system.

The housing system increasingly comprised of residualised public housing catering for a much narrower group of lower-income households and an ever growing private homeowning sector. While the private rental sector underwent little change in terms of size, conditions or regulation this would change as both the squeeze on the social housing sector and the expanding mortgage credit sector converged on the long-neglected tenure.

In 1988 the National Economic and Social Council (NESC) published a major review of housing policy, based on a detailed analysis of every aspect of the housing system, by John Blackwell from University College Dublin.

The Council's recommendations reaffirmed the status of 'owner occupation as socially desirable' arguing that 'it should be encouraged as the main housing tenure'.[21] Concern over the residualisation of social housing and the need to reduce public expenditure on owner-occupier supports were also key recommendations.

Significantly in their discussion of Local Authority Housing the issue of social 'polarisation' and 'segregation' was raised. The combined impact of the Surrender Grant, tenants purchase and the recession were all noted as causes of increased social-economic marginalisation of some

Council estates.[22] In response the Council suggested that
the

> practice of building large social segregated local
> authority and private housing estates should be
> discontinued, and local authorities should plan socially
> mixed communities by purchasing private houses
> for letting and building houses for letting in private
> estates.[23]

This and other recommendations were to have a significant
impact on the development of housing policy in the coming
decade.

A New Consensus

Two important developments at the end of the 1980s
were to set the tone for significant changes to housing
policy in the coming decade. The 1987 Programme for
National Recovery agreed by the Fianna Fáil government
was the first in a series of trilateral social partnership
agreements involving Government, trade unions and
business.

The core focus of this, and indeed subsequent
agreements, was pay and productivity, underpinned by
reducing public debt and stabilising the State's finances.
While social policy commitments were included, particularly
after the involvement of the community, voluntary and
environmental sectors, they were clearly secondary to and
dependent on the primary objective of generating economic
growth.

The social policy commitments of the 1987 agreement
were contained in a section titled Greater Social Equity and

detailed twenty-two actions across social welfare, health, education and housing. The fact that there were just two commitments on housing policy indicated where it lay in the social partners' priorities. The agreement included a promise to introduce new legislation dealing with homelessness and a 'special emphasis ... to be given to the housing needs of disadvantaged groups'.

The following year saw the passing of the Housing (Miscellaneous Provisions) Act 1988 which provided for the first time a statutory definition of homelessness and created a dedicated stream of funding for Councils and Approved Housing Bodies (AHB) to provide accommodation and supports for people experiencing homelessness. The Act also introduced a new requirement on Local Authorities to produce triennial social housing needs assessments and social housing plans.

However, the real shift in housing policy came with the publication in 1991 of *A Plan for Social Housing* by the Department of Environment. This was the first major statement of Government housing policy since the 1969 Department of Local Government document, *Housing in the Seventies.*

The 1991 plan set out an overarching approach for housing policy underpinned by the significant changes to funding and provision that took place during the previous decade. While heavily influenced by the 1988 NESC report, it lacked much of the earlier document's nuance. Crucially it laid the foundations of a policy consensus that has informed almost all Government housing policy since.

The plan sets out three key objectives: 'promoting owner occupation as the form of tenure preferred by most people; developing and implementing responses appropriate to changing social housing needs, [and] mitigating the extent and effects of social segregation in housing'.[24] It promised to 'introduce a range of new measures to deal with social housing need' which were expected to 'improve housing prospects and [grant] quicker access to housing for people of limited means' as well as ensure 'a more efficient and equitable use of resources, improved opportunities for community and voluntary action in housing [and] more choice in housing'.[25]

The document exuded a certain optimism detailing that, according to the first Housing Needs Assessment carried out under the 1988 Act, there were just 19,000 households in need of social housing and that 1990 saw the first increase in capital spending for social housing since 1984.

To meet this housing need the plan promised 'a range of complimentary and innovative measures that will reduce the traditional degree of dependence on local authority housing'.[26] Crucially the document asserted that 'The resumption of house building by local authorities on the scale of the early to mid-eighties ... would not now be appropriate.'[27] This was a very narrow interpretation of the NESC recommendation on the need to counteract class segregation.

The significant policy shift was justified as being 'in line with the international trend which is away from the direct provision of housing by public authorities' and was designed to avoid 'reinforced social segregation' which was deemed to have been a feature of the more traditional approach to social housing provision.

While clearly the primary rationale for this new diversification was fiscal, i.e. avoiding a return to large-scale capital expenditure, the 1991 Plan was the first occasion in which the policy objective of promoting 'a better social mix' was clearly set out.[28]

To achieve these objectives the plan outlined a twin track approach of improved capital spending for direct Local Authority building to increase output in 1991, alongside a medium-term target for the new delivery streams to reach 5,000 social housing units a year. However, it was estimated that these new streams would initially deliver just 750 homes in 1991 and within three years reach the 5,000 target.

Central to these new delivery streams was an enhanced role for Approved Housing Bodies. Up until that point the role of the not-for-profit sector was extremely limited. Government capital funding for special needs housing, targeting older people and those experiencing homelessness, was first provided in 1984. By 1991 a total of 1,600 units of such accommodation had been provided.

The *Plan for Social Housing* introduced for the first time a funding mechanism that would allow Approved Housing Bodies to provide general needs housing similar to Councils. The Rental Subsidy Scheme, later to be renamed the Capital Loan Subsidy Scheme, would provide loans to Housing Associations to build or buy properties and a rental subsidy for housing a waiting list applicant, which over thirty years would repay the loan.

Interestingly for a document titled *A Plan for Social Housing*, though not surprising given the Government's privileging homeownership, the plan also included a range of measures to promote even greater levels of owner-occupation. Again, the optimism was evident in the self-acknowledgement that 'we have succeeded in achieving one of the highest levels of owner occupation in the world (80%)' but recognised that 'there remain households, especially younger people, who have an unrealised strong ambition to own their own homes'.[29]

To rectify this a new shared ownership scheme was to be introduced in the following years with the Council co-owning 50 percent of the home on which the owner would pay rent and ultimately buy out the State's equity after twenty-five years.

There was also a new £3,300 mortgage allowance for Council tenants who surrendered their tenancy in order to purchase a private house. Though similar to the discredited 1984 Surrender Grant the plan suggested that as it was not 'a direct cash grant, the new allowance should not result in the large scale surrender' and that it would be 'monitored to ensure that it does not adversely affect the social stability of local authority estates'.[30]

There were also modest measures providing loans for house purchase and refurbishment and funds to allow Local Authorities to sell land for the building of affordable homes.

The plan also contained explicit references to homelessness, Travellers and the private rented sector, areas of housing policy ignored in previous decades.

The section on homelessness expressed some concern that Local Authorities were not fully implementing their new powers under the terms of the 1988 Act. In response they would be required to provide a full assessment of the need for accommodation for homeless people by mid-1991 and to report to the Minister directly with respect to progress in accessing the new Section 10 funding for emergency accommodation provision.

It was also interesting that the plan accepted the need to provide Travellers with serviced caravan parks rather than force people into standard social housing, and provided £3 million in capital funding for this purpose.

The private rented sector clearly remained the least regulated and least favoured tenure in the plan. This was hardly surprising, though, given that the sector was in decline at just 9 percent of the total housing stock in 1991.

A review of the sector by the Department had concluded and recommended action on a number of fronts though emphasised 'the need to ensure that any measure being considered would not adversely affect the supply of private rented accommodation or act as a disincentive to new investment'. The proposed regulations dealing with rent books, letting agreements, minimum standards and notices to quit would be dealt with in future legislation.

The report also promoted the benefit of Section 23 tax reliefs as an incentive to encourage investment in future private rental supply despite the low take up since their introduction in 1988.

The significance of *A Plan for Social Housing* cannot be underestimated. It set out a broad policy framework that has remained in place ever since. Traditional social housing delivery by Local Authorities would continue but on a much smaller scale. This would be complemented with the entry of the Approved Housing Body sector into mainstream social housing and a number of affordable housing schemes.

Despite the document's optimism, delivery during the 1990s was less than expected. Local Authorities fell short of their 1,500 target for 1991 delivering just 1,180 units. They gradually brought the annual output up to 3,713 homes in 1999 delivering a total of 25,000 homes during the decade, the lowest level of output since the lean 1940s.[31]

Meanwhile the great promise of the Approved Housing Body sector proved an even bigger disappointment. Just

2,136 homes were delivered for general needs housing under the Rent Subsidy/Capital Loan Subsidy Scheme between 1991 and 1999, with an annual average output of 267 units. The special needs housing, funded under the Capital Assistance Scheme, targeting older people, those with disabilities and those exiting homelessness, performed slightly better delivering 3,922 units over the decade, almost double the annual output of general needs housing.[32]

The modest Council and Approved Housing Body programme was unable to meet both existing and emerging need as the figures from the triennial Housing Needs Assessment clearly show. By 1993 the Council housing list had grown to 28,200 households and increased even further to 39,176 by 1999.[33]

Meanwhile the new affordable housing measures were also running into difficulty. Between 1991 and 2002, 29 percent of home purchases were facilitated by the schemes introduced under *A Plan for Social Housing*. However, as Norris notes, up to 38 percent of those participating ended up in mortgage arrears due to difficulties in meeting the high level of payments or paying down the Council's equity stake.[34]

While unforeseen at the time the schemes were introduced, house price inflation began to increase dramatically from 1996, affecting the genuine affordability of the measures. Norris notes that from 1990 to 1993 house prices increased by 8 percent per year. However, from 1996 to 2002 the average annual increase was 22 percent.[35]

Government published a housing policy review in 1995 titled *Social Housing, The Way Ahead*. In addition to assessing the delivery on the 1991 commitments the review sought to increase output to 7,000 units a year, a target not actually reached until 2005. It also brought a greater focus on issues of estate management and tenant participation while reaffirming once again private homeownership as the preferred tenure.[36]

As the decade came to a close it was clear that the promise of *A Plan for Social* Housing 'of ensuring that every household has a dwelling suitable to its needs, located in an acceptable environment, at a price or rent it can afford' remained unfulfilled. One of the consequences of the failure of the plan, and one completely unexpected at the time, was the dramatic increase in the number of social housing eligible households living in the private rented sector subsidised by the State.

Rent Supplement was introduced in 1977 as part of the supplementary welfare allowance scheme. Its purpose was to provide short-term emergency support to people unable to meet the cost of their own rents. During the 1980s expenditure on the payment was low. By 1990 the total spend was just over €10 million, at current prices. However, by 1995 the cost had spiralled to €69 million and continued rising to €127 million by 1999, an increase of an astonishing 1,170 percent in the decade.[37] During the 1980s the number of claimants rose from 1,316 in 1981 to 8,848 by 1987. However, by 1999 there were 41,873 households supported through Rent Supplement and an increasing number of them were accessing the payment on a long-term basis.[38]

What started out as a short-term income supplement had rapidly become a long-term social housing support meeting the housing needs of twice the number of households as was met by new Local Authorities and Approved Housing Bodies output during the decade. That there could be a relationship between the shift in housing policy away from large-scale Local Authority provision brought about by *A Plan for Social Housing* and the emergence of the subsidised private rental sector as a de facto social housing support was clearly not appreciated by policy makers at the time.

The most immediate consequence was a shift in the tenure balance in the State. For the first time in the twentieth century the percentage of owner-occupiers fell, albeit marginally from 79 percent in 1991 to 77.4 percent in 2002 (though the total number of private homeowners increased by 182,338 during the decade). Meanwhile the social rental sector declined marginally from 10 percent in 1991 to 9.8 percent in 2002 while the private rental sector rose from 9 percent to 12.7 percent during the same period.

As the millennium approached the Southern Irish housing system was set for a period of massive growth in investment and house building. So too in housing need as ever greater numbers of people were unable to access secure or affordable housing either from the private market or from Local Authorities and the Approved Housing Body sector.

House Prices Explode

The arrival of the Celtic Tiger economy can be measured against a number of indicators including rising levels of employment, increasing Gross Domestic Product and greater levels of consumer spending. However, given the centrality of housing to both the boom and subsequent bust, the arrival of double digit house price inflation is probably the best gauge of when the Tiger economy really started to roar.

Through the early years of the 1990s house price inflation and output were modest. Things started to change from 1995/96 when an increase of 11.8 percent was recorded. In the following three years the upward trajectory continued at 22.6 percent in 1996/97, 18.5 percent in 1997/98 and 13.9 percent in 1999/2000. While the following two years saw a dip back into single digits the upward surge returned from 2002/03. In 1994 the average price of a house in the State was €72,000. By 2004 it had soared to €249,000, an increase of 243 percent.[39] In 1997/98 Dublin witnessed an astonishing 32 percent increase in house prices.

The actual cost of this dramatic increase in value across the State, and particularly in the urban areas, was incredible. Average house prices in Dublin started at €81,000 in 1994, reached €160,000 by 1998 and continued rising until they reached €322,000 in 2004. In Limerick the corresponding figures were €68,000, €104,000 and €210,000. Even outside the cities, values increased dramatically from on average €66,000 in 1994 to €116,000 in 1998 and on to €228,000 in 2004.

Most of the rising cost of buying a home had little to do with the cost of building or labour. Michael Punch and P.J. Drudy note that during this period 'new house prices have increased over four times faster than house building costs and seven times faster than the consumer price index ...'.[40] The authors quote an *Economist* magazine index published in 2005 which showed that from 1997 to 2005 Ireland had the highest rate of increase in a survey of OECD countries at 192 percent, followed by Britain at 154 percent, Spain at 145 percent and Australia at 114 percent.[41] The article went on to show that such increases were not experienced in all countries with some such as the US and Canada witnessing more modest rises while others such as Hong Kong, Japan and Germany saw prices fall.

If the cost of materials or labour were not the key drivers of rising house prices then what accounted for the dramatic surge? Rising demand was obviously key. Nevertheless, the National Economic and Social Council noted that '35 per cent of all new dwellings in the recent past do not appear to lead to the formation of a new permanent household', indicating that a significant proportion of the increased demand was driven by investors rather than home buyers.[42]

Land costs were a key factor with the Irish Home Builders Association noting a 200 percent rise in the cost of sites in Dublin.[43] However, rising land values were themselves a function of decisions by investors armed with ever greater and cheaper sources of capital to invest in commercial and residential development rather than the productive economy.

While the first wave of financial liberalisation introduced in the United States, Britain and Ireland from the late 1970s and 1980s had little impact on residential investment in Ireland, the second wave of reform, introduced through the European Union in the early 1990s, was much more significant.

In 1993 the European Commission proposed a series of changes to banking regulation broadly in line with the Basel reforms of the 1970s. This increased standardisation of banking practices across the European Union coupled with the introduction of the Euro convergence criteria following the adoption of the Maastricht Treaty in 1992 brought about a significant reduction in interest rates. As Ryan-Collins notes, the 'increased competition from non-specialised mortgage lenders – not least large banks – put further pressure on rates'.[44]

The consequence of these changes for mortgage lending, and thus demand for new homes, was dramatic.

Ryan-Collins points out that

> European mortgage markets doubled in size in nominal
> term between 1990 and 2000. There was particularly
> explosive growth in Greece, Spain, Portugal, Ireland
> and the Netherlands, all of which experienced increases
> in outstanding mortgage loans of over 300 percent ...[45]

This expansion of mortgage credit was further fuelled
by the introduction of the Euro in 1999 which led to an
'explosion in capital market activity with the establishment
of a Euro-denominated bond market'.[46]

Banks and Governments further fuelled this tsunami of
investment into residential property. Back in power, Fianna
Fáil introduced a number of changes to the tax code in
the 1998 budget passed in November 1997 including the
abolition of the Residential Property Tax and reduction of
Capital Gains Tax to 20 percent. The consequence of these
measures against the backdrop of European Union-wide
financial liberalisation saw the single biggest hike in house
price inflation in the following twelve months.

Increased competition amongst banks led to changes to
the Loan-to-Value Ratio available to lenders, most famously
with the introduction of the 100 percent mortgage as well
as significantly longer maturities. The arrival of major
international players such as Bank of Scotland into the
Irish market in 2001 increased the pressure on domestic
lenders to follow these aggressive and high-risk practices.
The securitisation of mortgage lending and the creation of
secondary markets for these apparently low-risk financial
products further fuelled lending.

Mortgage lending as a percentage of Gross Domestic
Product rose dramatically, from 37 percent in 2000 to 72

percent by 2006. For five of the State's thirteen largest indigenous lenders the mortgage lending was 80 percent of their loan book.[47]

Bad decisions from Government and a failure of the Financial Regulator are clearly to blame for the scale of the residential property bubble that was allowed to grow from 1996 onwards. However, it is important to fully understand the broader European and Global context without which the dramatic house price inflation and the very serious social and economic consequences that came with it would not have happened.

Financial deregulation was driven by a desire to generate greater levels of profitability for investors at a time of slowing economic growth in the real economy. Increased lending, both to buy houses and to borrow against the rising value of your home to fund general consumer spending, was believed to be a credible solution to the economic slump of the late 1970s. Yet as we now know the level of risk contained within this debt-driven policy was considerable.

Ryan-Collins calls this the 'housing-finance feedback cycle' of which Ireland was a very extreme example. He explains that

> The combination of financial deregulation and innovation, increased expectation of future house price increases, greater opportunities for economic rent extraction via capital gains in land values, housing equity withdrawal, weakening real wages and welfare provision has proved a powerful mix.[48]

The long-term consequences of this financial-economic model will be discussed further below. Nevertheless, the most immediate impact was the incredible paradox of enormous numbers of houses being built between 1996 and 2008 while at the same time there were rising levels of housing need at rates not seen before, as both those waiting for social housing and those traditionally able to finance their own housing were unable to access affordable accommodation.

Ignoring Good Advice

In response to the growing crisis of housing affordability the National Economic and Social Council, a body with very significant influence during the era of social partnership, undertook a major assessment of the housing system. *Housing in Ireland, Performance and Policy* was published in 2004, and while its conclusions and recommendations were ultimately overtaken by the descent into recession from 2008 it is a document of enormous significance.

The 200-page assessment, supplemented by hundreds of pages of more detailed analysis in a series of background briefing papers, was the most substantial investigation of the housing system in the history of the State. While its muted tone was clearly a consequence of a document written by and reflective of the social partners, including Government, industry, unions and the community and voluntary sector, it nonetheless had some sharp observations and strong recommendations.

The report described the housing system as 'dynamic but unbalanced', highlighting 'the gap between demand and supply ... in inequality of opportunities and pressures across income groups and in the imbalance between the provision of private and social housing.'[49] These imbalances were undermining 'the economic, social and environmental sustainability of the settlements and neighbourhoods' then under construction, argued the report.[50]

While much of *Housing in Ireland* is descriptive, highlighting trends and possible risks, and many of its recommendations were general in nature, it did make some hard proposals. Most significantly it urged Government to increase the stock of social housing 'owned and managed by Local Authorities and approved housing bodies' to 200,000 by 2012. This would require a total additional provision of 73,000 units over eight years at an estimated capital cost of €1.4 billion per year.

The report also highlighted the growing affordability issues for both private renters and home buyers suggesting that 20 percent of renters were paying more than 35 percent (the Government's definition of affordability under the Planning and Development Act 2000) of their post-tax income on accommodation. While the picture for recent home buyers was less clear cut, the report did emphasise the risks inherent in the growing levels of mortgage debt, particularly if interest rates were to rise or wages fall.

Interestingly the report highlights three main concerns regarding the housing system, which while not shared by all members were a significant portent of things to come. In a section on the stability of the system the following observation was made:

> One group of observers consider that the Irish housing market displays a strong instability and irrationality, amounting to a 'bubble' that is likely to burst when the irrational expectations and exuberance that drives the market turn from positive to negative. Then, the upward spiral of asset values, wealth appreciation and demand will turn into a downward spiral of falling prices, negative equity and market withdrawal.[51]

While the report went on to note that 'more optimistic observers do not fear for the stability of the housing system' it is clear that the report's extensive support for greater provision of social and affordable housing was intended as both a warning of and a protection against the fear of recession.

The Council argued strongly for an increase in social housing output not just as a means for meeting social housing need but 'in view of the likely easing of private demand over time ... an increase in social housing output could contribute to the goal of delivering a soft landing for the housing sector'.[52]

The report's detailed discussion of the relative merits and risks of 'dualist' versus 'unitary' housing systems and its advocacy of cost rental as a means of both meeting affordable housing need and stabilising the system overall were far-reaching.[53]

Housing in Ireland stopped short of advocating a 'unitary' housing model closer to those of Germany, Austria and some Scandinavian countries. And though some of its less controversial recommendations were taken up by Government its two key proposals – a dramatic increase in real social housing and the use of not-for-profit or low-profit cost rental affordable accommodation (to meet the needs of households above the income thresholds for social housing but unable to afford private housing) were ignored.

In December 2005 the Department of Environment issued a short three-page Housing Policy Framework statement entitled *Building Sustainable Communities*. Acknowledging NESC's *Housing in Ireland* report it promised a more detailed document in 2006. However, the core principles of the 2005 statement indicated little change in direction and no recognition of the anxieties and risks explored in the NESC report.

Building Sustainable Communities spoke of 'huge advances in the past decade' in housing delivery as 'overall supply of houses has increased dramatically' and 'more social and affordable housing, and improved options for accessing this kind of accommodation, have been made available to people'.[54]

Twice the document emphasised Government's 'key objective ... to promote the conditions whereby the maximum number of people can access accommodation through private provision' and that 'home ownership should be available to as many people as possible where this is their preferred option ... [as] ... Homeownership can be an important factor in underpinning social stability and promoting good civic values.'[55]

It is hard not to draw the implication that Government believed other tenures and in particular social and private rental did not lend themselves to social stability and good civic values and thus actively pursued a policy of downgrading these tenures in preference of private homeownership.

Instead the Policy Statement promised the delivery of a number of measures that would assist people's access to private sector housing at more affordable prices. Meanwhile the NESC target of 73,000 additional social houses over twelve years was ignored. Instead there was a lower and shorter commitment to fund the provision of 23,000 homes by Councils and Approved Housing Bodies in 2006, 2007 and 2008.

The social housing targets were 20 percent short of the NESC requirement of 9,125 new homes a year though the Government came within a few hundred units of their own target, delivering 22,622 over the three years.

Despite this, overall social housing need continued to rise with the number of households on Council waiting lists increasing by 30 percent from 42,946 households in 2005 to 56,249 households in 2008.

The number of households in subsidised private rental accommodation also increased significantly during this period as Rent Supplement claims rose from 60,176 in 2005 to 74,038 in 2008.

In response to the escalating cost of Rent Supplement the Department of Social Welfare and Department of Environment agreed that from 2005 long-term recipients of the social welfare payment (those in payment more than eighteen months) would transfer to a new payment managed by Local Authorities called the Rental Accommodation Scheme (RAS).

RAS was officially seen as a long-term social housing support with a number of advantages to the tenant and landlord including four-year leases, rent paid directly by the Council to the owner, and tenants paying a differential rent to the Council and thus able to take up employment and increase income without losing any entitlement to the scheme.

However, RAS was still a subsidy to a private sector landlord and a short-term tenant support rather than a long-term social housing allocation. The inclusion of RAS tenancies in the legal definition of social housing in the Housing (Miscellaneous Provisions) Act 2009 resulted in tenants losing their place on the Councils' principal housing list and restricting future transfers to within the RAS housing stock only. In 2005 there were 606 RAS tenancies. By 2008 this had increased to 6,915.

Thus the total number of social housing applicants living in subsidised private rental accommodation in 2008 was 81,053 households at a cost of €393,573. While both the Rent Supplement and Rental Accommodation Schemes may have been designed for a different purpose, they had become an alternative mechanism for meeting social housing need. This was part of a broader shift in social housing provision in many countries described as a move 'from bricks to benefit' by British writer Anna Minton in her book on the housing crisis in London describing a similar phenomenon.

Meanwhile the number of new houses (public and private) being built continued to rise. In 1991 approximately 19,000 new homes were added to the stock. By 1996 the annual output had reached 33,725. Within a decade output would treble with an astonishing 93,000 homes being built in a single year.[56] Yet despite ever increasing levels of supply, house prices, rents, social housing waiting lists and rent subsidy dependency levels were all increasing.

Speculative investment in property was creating ever greater levels of instability and irrationality making the housing system increasingly dysfunctional and driving the very inequality and unsustainability that the 2004 NESC report warned against.[57] Indeed, so intoxicated with their own economic and electoral success, the Fianna Fáil Government led by Bertie Ahern continued to ignore advice they themselves commissioned which, if followed, would have gone some way to temper the irrational exuberance of the Celtic Tiger bubble.

The Government funded three reports by property consultants Bacon and Associates in 1998, 1999 and 2000 to advise on how best to respond to the bullish property market. Norris notes that despite the Bacon reports highlighting 'the role which speculative demand for housing from property investors played in driving house price inflation' and recommending 'a number of measures to control this demand' including abolition of Mortgage

Interest Tax Relief to landlords and an anti-speculative tax, the Government took neither course of action.[58]

As private homeownership became increasingly out of reach of young working households this added to the pressure on the private rented sector, leading to significant increases in rents. While the Government had introduced a number of weak rental sector regulations in the Housing (Miscellaneous Provisions) Act 1992 in line with the commitments set out in *A Plan for Social Housing*, the sector remained very much the same as the 1990s came to a close.

Nevertheless, as the sector began to grow, and in light of problems with low standards and high rents, Government established a Commission on the Private Rental Sector to examine how security of tenure could be improved while maintaining a 'reasonable balance between the respective rights and obligations of landlords and tenant'. The Commission included representation from tenant and landlord interests and examined issues of tenure, rent setting and dispute resolution.

However, very significant differences of opinion between the sectors resulted in strong criticism of the report's final recommendations from both Threshold and the Irish Property Owners Association. Published in 2000 the Commission recommended a limited security of tenure, a market-based rent review mechanism and the establishment of a Residential Tenancies Board (RTB) which would register tenancies and resolve landlord-tenant disputes.

Threshold responded by arguing that

The range of recommendations proposed by the Commission in relation to security of tenure, rent

regulation and affordability will not result in a
fundamental and necessary reform of the private rented
sector and will not result in a substantial immediate
benefit to tenants. The absence of any proposals for rent
regulation is an inadequate response where significant
numbers of tenants face substantial rent increases.[59]

Meanwhile the Irish Property Owners Association claimed
the tenancy protections were in breach of investors' property
rights and 'will be open to abuse by unscrupulous tenants'
while the requirement to register and the powers of the
Residential Tenancies Board 'constituted an unreasonable
burden on landlords'.[60]

Disagreements notwithstanding the subsequent Residential Tenancies Act 2004 was broadly in line with the
Commission's recommendations providing tenants with four-
year tenancies subject to a six-month probationary period,
regulations regarding issuing of notices of terminations,
market-based rent reviews and a registration and dispute
resolution board which came into operation in 2005.

By 2002 the number of private rental properties across
the State had risen to 141,000 (from 81,000 in 1991). In
total, almost 13 percent of households were now renters
with 39 percent of Dublin residents residing in the private
rental sector.

Despite this growth and the new regulation of the
sector, Government's eyes remained firmly on owner-
occupation. Their promised substantive *Housing Policy
Statement* was published in February 2007 and set out a
more detailed and in some respects more ambitious plan
than contained in the 2005 document.

Delivering Homes, Sustaining Communities was a ninety-
page statement on housing policy setting out in some detail

how the Government intended to deal with the housing system for the period up to 2013. While the principle focus remained on homeownership there were also sections dealing with planning, urban design and service provision as argued for in the 2004 NESC *Housing in Ireland* report.

It also set out a programme for social and affordable housing delivery, with a significant emphasis on the use of both the Rental Accommodation Scheme and the Part V provisions of the Planning and Development Act 2000 requiring private developers to provide 20 percent of all new housing (or the equivalent in land or cash) for social and affordable use.

The plan promised to meet the social housing needs of 100,000 households by 2013 with 40,000 Council, Approved Housing Body and RAS units to be delivered by 2009. It also committed to 40,000 affordable homes to be delivered over the same period with an initial allocation of 17,000 by 2009.

Delivering Homes, Sustaining Communities also included a range of Local Government reforms and a renewed focus on tackling homelessness, for the first time setting a formal date of 2010 by which long-term homelessness and the need to sleep rough would end.

The subsequent Housing (Miscellaneous Provisions) Act 2009 required Councils to produce housing action plans and detail how they would deliver on the 2010 homeless target. Most significantly, and for the first time, the Act provided for a statutory definition of social housing including not just houses owned by Local Authorities and Approved Housing Bodies but tenancies funded under the Rental Accommodation Scheme.

The justification for formally classifying subsidised private rental tenancies as a form of social housing was grounded in a 2005 NESC report *The Developmental Welfare State* which called for more 'flexible' supports to take account of the different needs of households during their 'life cycle'. However, for Government the real attraction of the shift to current expenditure supports was financial as it allowed them to claim higher levels of annual social housing delivery at a greatly reduced cost.

From the enactment of this section of the legislation in 2010, households in RAS accommodation were deemed to have their long-term housing needs met and were removed from the Councils' principal housing list.

Social housing and RAS commitments came in just ahead of target by 2009 with 22,361 units delivered by Local Authorities and Approved Housing Bodies and 19,771 RAS tenancies created. However, it is important to note that the RAS tenancies were not new accommodations but Rent Supplement claimants remaining in their existing accommodation but transferring the rental subsidy from the Department of Social Welfare to the Local Authority. Nonetheless, the Government could claim to have met the target set out in *Delivering Homes, Sustaining Communities*.

On the affordable front, however, the output was significantly off target with just 45 percent of the proposed 17,000 homes delivered. While Part V delivery was underwhelming on the social housing front it provided 5,000 affordable homes.

This level of output was not matched by either of the Government's affordable housing schemes with Shared Ownership delivering just 591 units over three years while the Affordable Housing Scheme delivered 2,075. In total 7,666 affordable homes were provided though many contained a significant risk of mortgage arrears if interest rates rose or the economy were to turn and unemployment increase. Rising house prices were putting even so-called affordable housing out of reach of working households on modest incomes.

As with the social housing targets set out in *A Plan for Social Housing*, the *Delivering Homes, Sustaining Communities* targets were not ambitious enough to meet either current or emerging housing need. The 2008 Housing Needs Assessment showed a further rise in the number of households on Council waiting lists to 56,249, a 30 percent increase on the 2005 assessment.

Meanwhile the cost of rental subsidies had increased to €595 million by 2009 as the number of Rent Supplement claimants soared to 93,030 in addition to the 6,802 RAS tenancies.

The policy and legislative initiatives from the mid-2000s were informed by what former senior Department of Environment official Eddie Lewis calls the Social Housing Reform Agenda. At the core of this agenda, according to Lewis, was

- The rejection of the idea of a house for life
- More choice for consumers
- The promotion of sustainable communities and a rejection of large, mono-tenure estates
- Greater standardisation in housing services
- A new regulatory framework for all rental accommodation
- A move towards tenure neutrality
- A housing-led response to homelessness.[61]

While Lewis argues that this approach marked a break from what he calls the 'traditional model' of social housing delivery, it is broadly a restatement of the policy consensus that had been in place since the 1991 *Plan for Social Housing*. The only real innovation was a commitment to tenure neutrality, but in the absence of measures to strengthen the social and private rental sectors, this would remain purely rhetorical.

There was clearly a mismatch between the commitment set out by Minister for Environment Dick Roche in his introduction to *Delivering Homes* to 'meet individual accommodation needs in a manner that facilitates and empowers personal choice and autonomy' and the targets agreed to meet this ambition.[62] Three years into their new plan it was clear to many that the Government's housing policy wasn't working, and things were about to get a whole lot worse.

The Housing Bubble Bursts

On the basis of the growing gap between need and delivery it is doubtful whether the Government's social and affordable housing plan as detailed in *Delivering Homes, Sustaining Communities* would have succeeded if the economy had continued to grow. However, the depth of the property crash that engulfed the economy and society from 2008 and the resulting imposition of sharp austerity policies first by Fianna Fáil and the Green Party from 2008 to 2010 and then by Fine Gael and Labour from 2011 onwards meant that the gap between housing need and supply would grow to levels previously thought unimaginable.

The story of the Great Crash of 2008 and the role property speculation and high-risk mortgage lending played in the collapse of the Celtic Tiger have been told elsewhere, most notably by Peadar Kirby (2010) and Seán Ó Riain (2014). For housing policy, the implications were profound, for very many real people they were devastating.

The most immediate effect was a dramatic reduction in private sector investment and Government capital spending on new housing. The private sector, crippled by the collapse of bank lending and the dramatic devaluation of their own assets, virtually ceased development overnight. Indeed, for some time the overhang of properties, built in areas people didn't want to live or at prices people couldn't afford, meant that ghost estates became among the first iconic images of the Crash.

The four Fianna Fáil austerity budgets of October 2008, April 2009, December 2009 and December 2010 were to see capital expenditure in social and affordable housing slashed from €1.5 billion in 2008 to €485 million in 2011. The result was an 80 percent drop in the output of social housing from 7,588 units in 2008 to just 1,564 in 2011.

As rising unemployment and the onset of significant mortgage distress dramatically increased the level of need for social housing and social welfare support, current expenditure on housing rose from €493 million in 2008 to €632 million by 2011. The number of households in subsidised private rental accommodation funded via Rent Supplement and RAS increased to 102,467.[63] Almost as many people were living in State-supported private rental accommodation as were living in Local Authority-owned social housing.

While the signing of the bank bailout deal with the Troika in 2010 served to stabilise the spiralling Government debt and deficit, capital expenditure continued to be cut even after the change of Government to a new Fine Gael and Labour coalition.

The promise of both parties to renegotiate the Troika deal proved to be one of many empty pre-election slogans. As a result, investment in social housing continued to decline to €397 million in 2012, €295 million in 2013 and €299 million in 2014. In turn, housing output plummeted with 1,391 homes delivered by Councils and Approved Bodies in 2012, falling to 757 in 2013 and 642 in 2014, even lower than the historic nadir of 769 units delivered in 1989.

The 2013 Housing Needs Assessment indicated a fall in the number of households on Council waiting lists to 89,872 with a corresponding drop in the numbers claiming Rent Supplement to 71,533 in the same year.[64] However these apparent declines were explained by the significant number of transfers from Rent Supplement to RAS and the removal of many of these households from the Council housing lists post-2010. Given that by 2013 there were 20,173 households in the Rental Accommodation Scheme, then the real comparison with the 2011 figures was a total social housing need of 110,045, an increase of 12 percent.[65]

Needless to say, the Government's deadline of 2010 for ending long-term homelessness and the need to sleep rough wasn't met as the number of people in emergency accommodation remained static. More worryingly homeless service providers started to notice an increase in economic homelessness, caused by the inability of working families to meet rental or mortgage payments.

On the policy front the new Minister for Housing, Fine Gael's Phil Hogan, and his Labour Party Minister of State with responsibility for Housing Jan O'Sullivan, released a *Housing Policy Statement* in June 2011. The optimistic and almost self-congratulatory language of Fianna Fáil's 2007 *Delivering Homes, Sustaining Communities* was replaced by a humbler tone. The short statement acknowledged that the 'over stimulation of the housing market is accepted as a key causal factor in the scale of the economic downturn.'[66] With the painful benefit of hindsight the document's authors were siding with the critical voices informing the 2004 NESC report by concluding that

> In a climate of low interest rates and rising incomes, a series of disastrous pro-cyclical policies led to a model that provided unprecedented growth, but it was a growth based not on foreign demand for our goods and services – as should be the case in a small open economy – or the productive use of investment capital to create sustainable employment. It was based on a mirage and a false assumption that the normal rules of supply and demand somehow did not apply in Ireland.[67]

The statement lamented 'the consequences of encouraging people to choose their housing options on the basis of investment and yield rather than hearth and home' and called for a 'a new vision for the sector' as fundamental to any economic recovery.

In outlining the basis of that vision, the statement proposed a significant departure which is worth quoting at length. In an explicit criticism of decades of privileging owner-occupation and downgrading social and private rental, its authors argued that

> Housing in Ireland has been characterised by a persistently hierarchical structure for several decades. This paradigm of housing has private home ownership at the top, with supported home-ownership (tenant purchase of local authority housing,

affordable housing) next, self-financed private rented accommodation further down, and State supported rental accommodation at the bottom (rent supplement/ social housing tenancies).

This structure and the value judgement that underlies it – which implicitly holds that the tenure which must ultimately be aspired to is homeownership – has had a considerable role in leading the Irish housing sector, Irish economy, and the wider Irish society to where they are today.

Our vision for the future of the housing sector in Ireland is based on choice, fairness, equity across tenures and on delivering quality outcomes for the resources invested. The overall strategic objective will be to enable all households access good quality housing appropriate to household circumstances and in their particular community of choice.[68]

Never before or since has a Government-sanctioned Housing Policy Statement made such a far-reaching critique of the prioritising of homeownership and the social-economic impacts that such a policy has had on the stability of the housing system.

However, as quickly as this rhetorical comment to tenure neutrality is made it is undermined both by an admission that 'home ownership will continue to be a significant feature of housing in Ireland and is likely to continue to be the tenure of choice for the majority of households'. The remainder of the statement reads not unlike the 'range of complimentary and innovative measures' promised in the 1991 statement *A Plan for Social Housing*.

The *Housing Policy Statement* ruled out 'a return to very large capital-funded construction programmes by local authorities' though on this occasion the constraints were explicitly fiscal rather than an adherence to 'international trends' or a desire to 'promote social mix'. Instead Government recommitted to using Approved Housing Bodies alongside a further reform of rent subsidies and the introduction of current expenditure to fund long-term leasing to meet social housing need.

There were also some modest commitments to further regulate the private rental sector, particularly focusing on how best to reduce the levels of deposit retention by landlords (which at that point was consuming a disproportionate amount of Residential Tenancy Board dispute resolution time) as well as measures to address homelessness, included as a recommitment to the Housing First model.

What is striking about the document is its failure to understand that private homeownership will only remain the tenure of choice if other tenures such as social rental, cost rental or private rental are less available or less secure. Promising 'choice, fairness and equity across tenures' is only meaningful if there is a level of investment and greater regulation of these long-neglected forms of accommodation that make them a viable option for those seeking a home.

Given that the Policy Statement made clear that its ability to engage in large-scale public housing expenditure was restrained by the recession, the real question was not what impact the document would have in the short term, but whether when increased financial resources did become available would the commitment to a tenure neutral housing system be acted upon.

In parallel to the *Housing Policy Statement* the Department of Environment also issued a revised *Homeless Policy Statement* later in 2011. In the main the document was a restatement of the approach outlined in two earlier homeless policies, *Homelessness, An Integration Strategy* of 2000 and *The Way Home, A Strategy to End Adult Homelessness* published in 2008. However, a new date of 2016 was set for the ending of long-term homelessness. How this target and indeed broader housing need would be met within the restrained budgetary limits imposed by the policies of austerity was not at all clear.

Social Housing Strategy 2020

The most significant housing policy innovations of the Fine Gael–Labour Government were born of self-imposed necessity. The constraints on capital expenditure led the Government to explore a range of complex current expenditure mechanisms for funding social housing. Alongside these, the review of Rent Supplement and the Rental Accommodation Scheme promised in the 2011 Policy Statement resulted in a new scheme introduced in the Housing (Miscellaneous Provisions) Bill 2014.

Alongside changes to Councils' legal powers to deal with anti-social behaviour and a new tenant purchase scheme the Housing Assistance Payment was the main feature of the 2014 Act. It was in principal the same as the RAS scheme but with a number of features more favourable to landlords including a lower inspection requirement, a shorter lease term (two years instead of the RAS four-year term) and a higher level of rent. The changes were justified on the basis of the lower than expected take up of RAS since its introduction in 2005.

The increased use of current expenditure to fund social housing and a renewed ambition to transfer all long-term Rent Supplement claimants onto HAP were central elements of the Government post-recession *Social Housing Strategy 2020* published by the new Minister for Environment, Labour's Alan Kelly, in 2014.

The plan promised to 'accommodate 90,000 households, the entire Housing Waiting List by 2020'.[69] This was to be achieved through the delivery of 35,000 social homes and 75,000 HAP and RAS tenancies. While the strategy promised to restore 'the State to a central role in the direct provision of social housing' this was to be achieved through the 'development of innovative funding mechanisms' that would be 'financially sustainable to meet current and future demand, ensuring value for money for the taxpayer while respecting the preferences of individual households to the greatest possible extent'.[70]

Before looking at the detail of how *Social Housing Strategy 2020* planned to meet these targets it is worth comparing them with that of their predecessor, the 2007 *Delivering Homes, Sustaining Communities*. The earlier plan promised 63,000 social houses to be built and bought by Councils and Approved Housing Bodies and 37,000 subsidised private sector tenancies to be funded via RAS over six years. *Social Housing Strategy 2020* reverses this 70:30 ratio in favour of real social housing with a commitment to 75,000 subsidised rental tenancies and just 35,000 social homes.

In 2014 the total stock of social housing was 132,200 units of which Councils owned 112,000 with Approved Housing Bodies controlling the remaining 20,200. Given that in 2004 the landmark National Economic and Social Research Council recommended increasing the stock 'of permanent social housing units owned and managed by local authorities and voluntary and cooperative housing bodies' to 200,000 by 2012, the lack of ambition in *Social Housing Strategy 2020* is clear. Even if the new plan met its targets it would still be 32,000 units short of the NESC recommendation by 2020, by which date overall social housing need would be significantly higher than that projected by NESC for 2012.

Not only was the strategy increasingly reliant on the private sector to deliver units for rental subsidies, but of the 35,000 units to be delivered by Councils and Housing Associations just 12,273 would be built and bought. The remaining 23,400 would be procured through a variety of current expenditure mechanisms, an unspecified number of which would permanently remain in the ownership of the private sector.

While the State may have a central role, it would increasingly be as a funder of subsidised leased private sector properties whether for two years under HAP, four years under RAS or ten years-plus on the long-term leasing schemes.

Further detail of the shift to current expenditure and long-term leasing was provided in Section 4 of the strategy. Within the National Asset Management Agency (NAMA, the State's bad bank dealing the legacy toxic debts from the Celtic Tiger era) was a special purpose vehicle called National Asset Residential Property Services (NARPS). This off-balance sheet entity had been used to lease vacant properties whose debts were on NAMA's books to Approved Housing Bodies. This vehicle was to be used to lease further properties for social housing use, with the State paying the lease for ten to twenty years while the property remained in the ownership of NARPS. A second off-balance vehicle was to be created with a fund of €400 million with which it was hoped it could leverage in addition funds for assisting Approved Housing Bodies to lease or purchase units.

Public Private Partnerships were also set to make a return, despite the high-profile collapse of a number of regeneration schemes in inner city Dublin during the crash. These were to deliver 1,500 units which at the end of a 25-year contract would be transferred into the ownership of Local Authorities.

The complexity of these new funding mechanisms alongside the requirements for 'commercial sensitivity' meant that it was impossible to establish whether they represented value for money for the taxpayer or the degree of contractual risk being carried by the State should something go wrong.

Crucially, as many would not be specifically provided for social housing use but, like RAS and HAP, taken out of the general stock of private sector properties for rent or purchase, there were concerns about both the lack of long-term security of tenure for the social tenants and the broader impact on supply and cost for non-social housing applicants seeking to rent and buy.

The *Social Housing Strategy 2020* included a number of small innovations including a commitment to explore the viability of cost rental affordable housing through a pilot scheme at the end of 2019, additional funding to get long-term vacant Council housing back into use and reforms of social housing allocations through the roll out of Choice Based Lettings and a facility to enable applicants to move from one Local Authority list to another without losing their accumulated years.

In the strategy's first full year of operation the results were underwhelming. Of the 15,786 social housing supports across the various streams just 10,786 were delivered, a shortfall of 33 percent. Significantly, the lowest level of output was in the delivery of social houses owned by Councils and Approved Housing Bodies, with just 1,580 of a promised 2,386 homes. The remainder of the 8,993 units were made up of privately rented or leased units (1,477 long term leases, 2,000 RAS tenancies and 5,860 HAP tenancies). In many cases these were not new tenancies, but simply a transfer of responsibility for the subsidy from one Government department to another.

One of the immediate consequences of this increasing reliance on the private rental sector to meet social housing need via increased RAS and new HAP targets was ever greater demand for rental properties pushing up prices across the sector. According to the Residential Tenancies Board Quarterly Rent Index rents declined sharply, particularly in Dublin, following the financial crash in 2008. Rents continued to fall through till 2010 and saw very modest increases from 2011 to 2013. However, rental inflation hit double digits from the second quarter in 2014 and continued to increase at that level though to 2015. While 2016 saw a slight moderation, the level of rental inflation was still above 6 percent annually.

The non-subsidised renters were being crowded out of the private rental sector by increasing numbers of social housing tenants. The worst affected were students and modest-income workers unable to access mortgage finance or first-time buyers saving for a deposit. The result was a perfect storm pushing rents to ever higher and unsustainable levels.

The immediate losers were low-income renters often on Rent Supplement with standard twelve-month contracts. With little protection from the existing rent review legislation introduced in 2004, which allowed rents to be raised annually in line with market rates, a new phenomenon started to take place. Families unable to meet the increased rents as their Rent Supplement payment was limited to a specified local ceiling that did not keep pace with rental inflation, were forced out of their existing accommodation.

In many cases this led to households presenting to their Local Authorities as homeless. In December 2014 there were 2,856 people officially recognised as homeless by the Department of Environment. By the following December that number had increased 27 percent to 3,625. However, the real increase was in the number of homeless families with children. In the twelve months from December 2014 the number of families in emergency accommodation jumped an astonishing 90 percent from 407 to 775 with 1,616 children homeless by December 2015.[71]

As the rental homeless crisis unfolded Housing Minister Alan Kelly desperately sought to convince the Fine Gael Finance Minister Michael Noonan to support him in introducing strong rent regulation. Kelly wanted to link rent increases to the Consumer Price Index, which at that point in time was close to zero. Noonan, a fiscal hawk, was steadfastly opposed to any such move arguing it would act as a disincentive to future investment in the private rental sector.

Noonan won what was, according to some accounts, a deeply acrimonious battle. Rather than genuine rent regulation, Kelly was reduced to introducing a Residential Tenancies (Amendment) Bill at the end of 2014 which would replace annual rent reviews with a review every second year alongside a longer lead time for the increased rents from 28 days to 90 days.

The highly respected homeless service provider and campaigner Fr Peter McVerry described the move as 'disastrous'. Speaking on RTÉ's *News at One* as the legislation was passing through the Oireachtas he said that between 60 and 70 families were becoming homeless every month:

> While families are flooding into homelessness, Government Ministers are bickering, arguing with one another and disagreeing with one another ... Nero fiddles while Rome burns – that's the only image we have. It's an absolute disgrace. We have a crisis, it's beyond crisis, we have an emergency.[72]

McVerry wryly told the news presenter that if there was a foot and mouth crisis affecting the beef industry the Taoiseach would summon his Ministers and have an emergency plan within forty-eight hours. A claim not without some justification.

Within three months a general election had been called and both the Fine Gael–Labour Government and with it *Social Housing Strategy 2020* were soon to be replaced. The election result was to return Fine Gael to office but the failure of the Labour Party to live up to many of its election promises and in particular the controversial role played by their Minister for Environment Alan Kelly in dealing with the issues of housing, homelessness and domestic water charges would see his party lose thirty seats, receiving their lowest share of the vote in their 100-year history.

The Dáil Housing and Homeless Committee

The 2016 general election was to provide an inconclusive result. The outgoing Government parties of Fine Gael and

Labour were the big losers with Enda Kenny's party losing 11 percent on their 2011 result and the Labour Party losing 13 percent. Fianna Fáil, despite its role in the economic collapse of 2008, made a modest and unexpected recovery, increasing their share by 7 percent. Meanwhile Sinn Féin took third place with 13 percent while the number of smaller parties and independents increased significantly. Despite the loss of seats, Fine Gael remained the largest party.

However, following initial talks with Fianna Fáil it was clear that a formal coalition Government would not be agreed. A series of interrupted engagements took place from April through till May before Fianna Fáil agreed to facilitate a minority administration as part of a 'confidence and supply' arrangement with Fine Gael. Enda Kenny was eventually elected Taoiseach in June with support from a small number of independents.

In April, while the talks were ongoing, Sinn Féin tabled a motion calling for the establishment of a temporary parliamentary committee to examine the deepening housing and homeless crisis. The motion was agreed and in the same month the Dáil Housing and Homeless Committee commenced six weeks of intense work, publishing a 153-page report in June.

The cross-party Committee met twice a week for six weeks, and took oral submissions from thirty-nine organisations in forty-one meetings lasting seventy hours. Presentations were made from individuals representing the Government, NGOs, industry, legal and academic sectors. There were also presentations from residents and individuals directly experiencing many of the issues under discussion. A further ninety written submissions were also submitted to the Committee for consideration.

The final report concluded that 'tackling the shortage of housing supply and the related problem of homelessness is one of the greatest challenges currently facing the country'.[73] Before outlining its key recommendations for Government the Committee offered its analysis of the causes of the current problem. The dramatic decline in social housing output since 2007 alongside the increased use of the private rental sector for social housing need had created problems both for social housing applicants and private renters. Demand for private rental accommodation was exceeding new supply and rents were increasing. Alongside this the recession and subsequent high levels of unemployment had left many homeowners in significant mortgage arrears.

The Committee also expressed concern that European Union fiscal rules were hampering the State's ability to invest to the appropriate level and that other sources of finance for house building such as the National Asset Management Agency and the Credit Union movement weren't being utilised. This, coupled with the high level of bureaucracy, meant that the volume and speed of social housing output was too low and too slow.

The Committee also expressed concern at the rise of homelessness among both those with complex needs and those rendered homeless by the crisis in the rental and mortgage sectors. There was also concern that some emergency accommodation was not suitable for the needs of individuals or families.

The report's priority recommendations were grouped into five sections dealing with social housing, the private rental sector, mortgage arrears, housing finance and homelessness and marked a significant departure from the core tenants of the *Social Housing Strategy 2020*.

The key proposal in the report was to 'increase the social housing stock (owned by local authorities and approved housing bodies) by at least 50,000 units (an annual average of 10,000 per year) through a programme of acquisition, refurbishment and new build'.[74] The definition of social housing was explicitly those units owned by the non-market sector and did not include subsidised rental tenancies such as HAP, RAS or long-term leasing as the Committee did not accept that these measures, while valuable as short- to medium-term supports, constituted long-term housing.

The rationale for this recommendation was twofold. Firstly, the Committee based its target on the 2004 NESC suggestion that the State needed a stock of 200,000 social housing units. Nevertheless, there was also considerable discussion on what a realistic delivery target would be, given the low level of output in the preceding years. The view of the majority of members was that while it would not be possible to reach 10,000 units in 2016 or 2017, a figure close to 8,000 was realistic which would be increased incrementally to ensure 50,000 units over five years.

To speed up the delivery of social housing the Committee also recommended reducing the length of time for the granting of Part 8 planning permissions, used for social housing developments, from eight to six weeks. This was complemented by the call for the creation of a Housing Procurement Agency to assist Local Authorities, many of whom had lost significant numbers of specialist staff during the recession, with technical support.[75]

The Committee was also concerned with the rising levels of family homelessness as a result of rent increases and mortgage distress in both the residential and buy-to-let sector. In response they called for the linking of rent reviews to an index such as the Consumer Price Index to halt the spiralling level of rent increases. In parallel to these measures the report urged Government to bring the Rent Supplement and Housing Assistance Payments in line with market rents.[76]

The Committee called for the introduction of a scheme for Councils and Approved Housing Bodies to purchase rental properties with the tenants remaining in situ (a Rent Switch programme); they voiced for an amendment to the Residential Tenancy Act to remove sale of property as grounds for issuing a Notice to Quit and to give tenants in such situations greater legal safeguards; they also called for a general improvement in the length of rental tenancies beyond the current four years.[77]

In June 2016 according to the Central Bank the total number of residential mortgages in arrears of more than ninety days was 52,571 while a further 14,828 buy-to-let mortgages were also in long-term distress.[78]

Their quarterly Mortgage Arrears and Repossession Statistics bulletin published that month recorded 1,783 residential dwellings in the bank's possession at the end of the quarter with a total of 397 properties transferring to the lenders in those three months, 101 via court order to repossess with the remaining 296 as a result of voluntary surrender or abandonment.[79]

The total number of buy-to-let properties that had been transferred into the management of receivers at the end of the quarter was 5,741 with 305 properties being transferred to the banks in that quarter, 171 via court ordered repossession and 134 via voluntary surrender or abandonment.[80]

The Housing and Homeless Committee urged the Government to introduce a legal moratorium on home repossessions and as a matter of urgency to bring forward a new plan to tackle the growing mortgage distress problem. The report called Government to make better use of a number of schemes to keep people in the family home including Mortgage to Rent, split mortgages, debt write downs and downsizing.[81]

There had been a considerable volume of discussion at the Committee on the issue of financing social and affordable housing delivery, particularly in the context of recent funding constraints caused by the policies of austerity and the changes to European Union fiscal rules following the adoption of the Treaty for Stability, Coordination and Governance (known by its critics as the Austerity Treaty) in 2013.

The final report contained a detailed section on financing and urged Government to provide 'the maximum possible direct Exchequer investment in the provision of social housing in the Capital Programme' alongside a call to 'urgently seek flexibility from the European Commission on the application of the EU fiscal rules for the financing of social housing'.[82]

The Committee also called on Government to make full use of Housing Finance Agency, Strategic Investment Fund and Credit Union lending to ramp up the delivery of social housing. There was also a clear demand for amendments to the 2010 NAMA Act to allow the State Agency 'to be an agent for the provision of social and affordable housing' and to 'use its cash reserves to tackle the housing and homeless crisis'.[83]

Finally, the Committee urged the incoming Minister with responsibility for housing to reinstate the policy of allocating 50 percent of social houses to households in emergency accommodation in Dublin, a policy introduced by the previous Minister Alan Kelly but allowed to lapse earlier in the year. This was accompanied by a demand not to close any emergency shelter while the crisis continued, to expand the availability of Housing First tenancies and to increase funding for the Health Service Executive for mental health supports for people experiencing homelessness.[84]

Mike Allen, the Director of Advocacy for Focus Ireland, one of the country's leading homeless charities, said that the Dáil Committee report set a 'benchmark' for the incoming Minister for Housing Simon Coveney. He welcomed the fact that the Committee members were 'very attentive to all submissions' and made 'substantial recommendations'. He told RTÉ's *Morning Ireland* radio programme that, 'We've been saying for years that homelessness needs to be a political priority – this [the Oireachtas Committee report] is what being a political priority looks like.'[85]

The report was published almost a month after Simon Coveney was appointed Minister for Housing and a month in advance of the publication of the Government's own housing plan. The decision of the new minority Fine Gael Government to split the Department of Environment in two and give Coveney, a senior figure in the new parliamentary party, responsibility for Housing, Planning and Local Government was a recognition of the depth of the housing crisis and the need for greater focus in resolving it. The big question was whether the new Minister and Government would listen to the all-party Dáil Housing and Homeless Committee and incorporate its recommendations into their plan.

New Minister, New Department, New Plan

The Fine Gael minority Government was actively supported by a number of independent Deputies and facilitated by

Fianna Fáil. In exchange for a number of policy agreements Micheál Martin's party would abstain on the election of Taoiseach, budget votes and any motions of no confidence.

The short written agreement between Fine Gael and Fianna Fáil included a section on housing entitled 'Securing affordable homes and tackling homelessness' which committed the incoming Government to a number of policies the most significant of which were to 'Significantly increase and expedite the delivery of social housing units, remove barriers to private housing supply and initiate an affordable housing scheme', 'Protect the family home and introduce additional long term solutions for mortgage arrears cases' and 'Provide greater protection for mortgage holders, tenants and SMEs whose loans have been transferred to non-regulated entities ('vulture funds').'[86]

Alongside this Fine Gael and their coalition partners in the Independent Alliance agreed to the Programme for Partnership Government including seven pages of commitments on housing and planning policy. The central proposal was for the new Minister for Housing to publish a detailed plan within 100 days of taking office. However, the programme also included a number of important commitments.

The issue of whether to enshrine the right to housing in the State's Constitution was to be referred to the new Oireachtas Housing Committee.[87] This was on foot of a 2014 recommendation of over 80 percent of participants of a Constitutional Convention established under the previous Government.

There was also a commitment, as with the *Social Housing Strategy 2020*, to develop an affordable cost rental stream of housing. The programme had an explicit promise to end the use of inappropriate hotel and BnB accommodation for homeless families.[88]

At the request of the Independent Alliance there was also a proposal to create a new statewide mortgage distress resolution service and a 'dedicated new court to sensitively and expeditiously handle mortgage arrears and other personal insolvency cases, including through imposing solutions, including those recommended by the new service'.[89]

On the day of his appointment as the State's first ever Minister for Housing, Simon Coveney tweeted: 'I'm privileged to be appointed as the new Minister for Housing, Planning and Local Govt. – Housing is the most urgent challenge for new Govt'. On 19 July ahead of schedule he published his plan.

The *Action Plan for Housing and Homelessness* subtitled *Rebuilding Ireland* was the longest housing plan of any Government in the history of the State. Running to 114 pages it had over ninety actions across five pillars: Address Homelessness, Accelerate Social Housing, Build More Homes, Improve the Rental Sector and Utilise Existing Housing.

In its Foreword the Taoiseach gave an early hostage to fortune promising to 'address fully and finally' the housing challenge. He repeated the Government's commitment to end the use of hotels and BnBs for homeless families and outlined a €5.5 billion allocation to underpin the implementation of the plan from 2016 to 2021. To demonstrate his own commitment to the plan he confirmed that he would personally chair a Cabinet Committee on Housing that would receive regular reports on its progress.[90]

The new Minister, in his Foreword, described the housing problems faced by people as 'an emergency situation' and outlined the plan's headline commitment of delivering 'a truly ambitious social housing programme of 47,000 units by 2021'. He also stated that his plan was 'informed, in particular, by the report of the Oireachtas Committee on Housing and Homelessness'.[91] The core objective of the plan was to

> ramp up delivery of housing from its under-supply across all tenures to help individuals and families meet their housing needs, and to help those who are currently housed to remain in their homes or to be provided with appropriate options of alternative accommodation.[92]

To this end the plan promised to facilitate the delivery of at least 25,000 new homes a year of which an average of 7,888 would be social homes. While the plan's five pillars contained eighty-plus action points, it identified forty-one of those as key actions.

Pillar 1 focused on homelessness. It promised that by 'mid-2017 hotels are only used in limited circumstances for emergency accommodation of families'.[93] This would be achieved by targeting 1,500 social homes for homeless families to be delivered by a Rapid Build Programme and a further 1,600 homes to be purchased by the Housing Agency. While the timescale for these two initiatives would be over three years, their initial output would result in a reduction of the number of homeless families within the first twelve months.

There was also a commitment to 'triple the targets for tenancies to be provided by Housing First teams in Dublin, from 100 tenancies currently to 300 tenancies in 2017'.[94] Other measures included more supports for homeless families and children to be delivered by Tusla, the Child and Family Agency, increases in Rent Supplement and the Housing Assistance Payment limits, and a new information service for people experiencing mortgage arrears and a reform of the Mortgage to Rent Scheme.

Pillar 2 dealt with the need to accelerate the delivery of social housing. The 47,000 social housing target would be delivered through three principal streams. Local Authorities and Approved Housing Bodies would build 26,000 homes and purchase a further 11,000 over the six years. Included in the build figure were direct builds, those purchased from private developers via Part V and an unspecified number of long-term vacant Council units that would be refurbished and brought back into stock.

The remainder would be made up of 10,000 privately owned units leased for ten to twenty years by Councils or Housing Associations.[95]

However, within those three principal streams would be a series of sub streams amounting to a complex web of delivery mechanisms. There was the Social Housing Investment Programme for Council construction, the Capital Assistance Scheme for special needs AHB construction, the Capital Advance Loan Facility for AHB construction, the Returning Vacant Properties to Productive Use for long-term voids and the Social Housing Current Expenditure Programme for long-term leased properties.[96] There was also standard Part V purchases and a smaller number of leased Part V units.

In addition to the 47,000 homes under the construction, acquisition and leasing programmes, *Rebuilding Ireland* also significantly expanded the *Social Housing Strategy 2020* targets for the Rental Accommodation Scheme and Housing Assistance Payment. Almost 90,000 households were to take up new HAP (83,270) and RAS (5,050) tenancies, some transferring from Rent Supplement and others moving directly from the waiting list to a subsidised tenancy.

Thus *Rebuilding Ireland* claimed it would meet the social housing needs of 135,810 households by 2021. Significantly only 37,000 of these would be in properties owned and managed by Local Authorities and Approved Housing Bodies. The remaining 98,810 households would be in privately owned properties subsidised by the State in two-, four- or ten-year-plus leases.

Pillar 2 also committed to develop a number of what were called Pathfinder Projects, selling public land to private sector consortia for the development of large-scale mixed tenure estates combining social, affordable and market price housing. There was also a proposal to streamline the approval and delivery process for social housing and to establish Housing Delivery and Procurement units within the Department of Housing. In line with previous policies the Approved Housing Body sector was to get an enhanced role. This was to be assisted with the development of an off-balance sheet funding vehicle. There were also measures to ensure that the housing needs of older people, those with disabilities and Travellers were met.

Pillar 3 introduced a range of mechanisms to assist private sector supply. Central to these were a number of grant aids and planning reforms that would reduce the cost and speed up the timeframe for the delivery of homes for private purchase.

A Local Infrastructure Housing Activation Fund (LIHAF) with an initial drawdown of €200 million was to be made available. Where a developer could demonstrate 'infrastructural impediments' in a specific development (i.e.

lack of funding for a road or bridge) and 'confirmation that the cost of providing that infrastructure by traditional means [i.e. from the developer's own resources] would make the provision of housing uneconomic/unaffordable/ restricted in number' then funding would be made available by Government.[97]

The purpose of LIHAF was not only to unlock private sector developments stalled for want of funds but to ensure the 'provision of housing at a lower price point' which would be affordable to those unable to access housing at open market prices.[98]

A fast-track planning process for developments of more than one hundred houses was promised alongside a new National Planning Framework to replace the old National Spatial Strategy. There were also some yet-to-be-defined 'land actions' and supports to promote 'efficient design and delivery methods to lower housing delivery costs' as well as 'measures to support construction innovation and skills'.[99]

The final two pillars dealing with the private rental sector and vacant homes were the least detailed. Pillar 4 promised a dedicated strategy for a 'viable and sustainable' rental sector along with additional powers for the Residential Tenancies Board and a review of rental standards. There was also a commitment for a cost rental scheme which was 'at an advanced stage of development and will be finalised by end of Q3 2016, for roll out by offer to potential housing providers thereafter'.[100] Reference was also made to a forthcoming student accommodation strategy to be developed by the Department of Education.

Similarly Pillar 5 promised the delivery of a strategy for tackling vacant homes, particularly in the private sector. Census 2016 estimated in excess of 183,312 vacant houses and apartments across the State. While subsequent estimates revised this figure downwards, there was no doubt that a large number of potential homes were lying vacant, particularly in inner cities and towns.

As part of this plan, funding was to be made available to Local Authorities to get more voids back into stock as well as three initiatives for privately owned vacant properties. €70 million was to be given to the Housing Agency to buy vacant properties from banks and funds, particularly for homeless families. The Repair and Lease scheme would assist owners of vacant properties with an upfront rent advance to assist with refurbishment costs in exchange for leasing the property back to the Council for a social tenant. The Buy and Renew Scheme would provide money directly to Councils to purchase vacant and often derelict homes to add to the general social housing stock.

The three schemes were to deliver 5,600 homes by 2021 with a Buy and Renew target of up to 500, a Housing Agency fund target of 1,600 and a Repair and Lease target of 3,500.

The response to the plan was mixed. Many commentators acknowledged the increased funding allocations as well as the more holistic approach to the housing system when compared with earlier plans. However, others expressed concern with the continued over-reliance on the private sector to deliver not just open-market-price homes but also social and affordable housing.

Conor Skehan, Chair of the Housing Agency, writing in *The Irish Times* following the launch of the plan said, 'These are exciting times' and that

> An innovative Government-wide initiative has begun, committing a huge part of our national resources to new ways of housing. If it succeeds we will not just

resolve a crisis, we will be enriched as a compassionate and efficient country. It must succeed.[101]

However, Fianna Fáil's housing spokesperson Barry Cowen indicated that his party was not 100 percent behind the plan telling RTÉ's *Drivetime* programme on the day of *Rebuilding Ireland*'s launch that

> There are gaps in this strategy that have to be filled. We will make proposals to fill them. In the event of them not doing so ... If, after that process is complete, we feel this Government cannot address this crisis we are going to have to look for another Government to do it.

Meanwhile Housing Policy expert Michelle Norris of UCD warned that meeting the proposed 25,000 new homes a year would be 'challenging' confirming the general view that whatever about the plan's promises the final judgement could only be made against what it actually delivered.[102]

Minister Coveney's Record – July 2016 to June 2017

In the months following the launch of *Rebuilding Ireland* the Taoiseach, Minister for Housing and other members of the Government repeated the claim that the *Action Plan for Housing and Homelessness* represented the single largest investment in social housing in the history of the State. To assess this claim, it is useful to compare it with its immediate predecessors.

Delivering Homes, Sustaining Communities promised 63,000 social houses and 37,000 subsidised rental tenancies through RAS in the period from 2007 to 2013. This would provide an average annual output of 9,000 social houses and 5,200 subsidised rental tenancies. The *Social Housing Strategy 2020* committed to 35,000 social houses and 75,000 subsidised rental tenancies over six years giving an annual average of 5,800 social and 12,500 rental tenancies. *Rebuilding Ireland* targets the delivery of 47,000 social and 82,000 subsidised rental tenancies over six years with an annual average of 7,800 social and 12,300 rental.

Both the 2014 and 2016 plans include long-term leased private units in their social housing figures. However, both the 2004 NESC report and the 2016 Dáil Housing and Homeless report explicitly described social housing as those units owned and managed by Local Authorities and Approved Housing Bodies. While there were no long-term lease targets included in the 2014 plan, *Rebuilding Ireland* includes 10,000.

There is a strong case for treating these leased units as part of the subsidised rental category rather than real social housing as the vast majority will remain in the ownership of the private sector when the lease term expires. On that basis the real breakdown in *Rebuilding Ireland* is 37,000 social and 98,000 subsidised private rental units with an annual average of 6,100 and 16,300 respectively.

Importantly, while *Delivering Homes, Sustaining Communities* included a target of 40,000 affordable homes over its seven-year life span, neither the *Social Housing Strategy 2020* nor *Rebuilding Ireland* include any targets for affordable homes, though nor did the 2004 NESC or 2016 Dáil Committee reports.

Two things stand out from this comparison. Firstly, the 2016 plan is broadly comparable with its immediate predecessor in social housing delivery but compares less well with the 2007 plan, which is more ambitious. Indeed, when set against both these plans and the significant expansion of social housing from 1948 or 1970 *Rebuilding Ireland* is not only unambitious, it is positively anaemic.

Secondly, when looking at the breakdown of social housing versus subsidised private tenancies the trend across all three plans is towards an increasing reliance on the private sector. *Delivering Homes* commits to meet the social housing needs of 100,000 households with 63 percent ending up in properties owned by Councils and Approved Housing Bodies. The *Social Housing Strategy* significantly reverses this ratio with 35 percent of households ending up in Council and AHB owned properties. The trend extends further in favour of the private rental sector with *Rebuilding Ireland* with just 27 percent of the total 135,000 social housing tenancies ending up in properties owned by Councils and Housing Associations.

Rebuilding Ireland also compares unfavourably with both the 2004 NESC report and the 2016 Dáil Committee report. The former called for 73,000 social houses, owned and managed by Councils and Approved Housing Bodies, to be delivered over eight years giving an average of 9,125 per year. The latter called for 10,000 units again owned and managed by Council and AHBs over a five-year period. Given that the 2004 report was published at a time of lower need and social housing output was low for much of the intervening period the Dáil Committee report acknowledged that the 10,000 annual target was a minimum to be exceeded.

It is hard to see how the *Rebuilding Ireland* social housing target meets with the Programme for Government Commitment or the Confidence and Supply Commitment to 'significantly increase and expedite the delivery of social housing units'. It certainly cannot be described as the biggest investment in social housing in the history of the State.

Given such modest commitments, it is not surprising that the Government met its targets in both 2016 and 2017. In 2016 the delivery of new build social housing was 700 homes ahead of target coming in at 2,965 units; acquisitions were also 200 ahead of target delivering 1,957 units. Likewise, each of the subsidised private streams were ahead with leasing delivering 792 units, 500 ahead of target. RAS came in 256 ahead of target with 1,000 units while HAP came in just over its target at 12,075 units.

In 2017 the Government exceed their targets by almost 5,000 units, requesting and securing a supplementary estimate of €100 million at the end of the year to cover the overrun. While new builds were slightly behind at 2,245, both voids and acquisitions were together 2,000 units ahead at 1,757 and 2,266 respectively. RAS came in just below target at 910 while leasing was just above at 798 and HAP almost 3,000 ahead of target at 17,916.

As *Rebuilding Ireland* was reaching its first anniversary, Minister Coveney was claiming to have met the social housing needs of 19,045 households in 2016 and was predicting to meet that of 25,000 households by the end of 2017. And yet housing need continued to rise.

The number of people officially classed as homeless by the Department of Housing increased from 3,256 adults and 1,318 children in June 2015 to 4,152 adults and 2,206 children in June 2016. By July 2017 when Minister Coveney left the department of Housing it had increased further to 5,187 adults and 2,973 children.[103] In his first year as Minister Simon Coveney presided over a 25 percent increase in adult homelessness and a 35 percent increase in child homelessness.

The occupation of Apollo House by Home Sweet Home, a coalition of housing activists, trade unions and cultural figures, in December 2016 became a focus for growing public anger at the homelessness scandal. The debts connected to the vacant city centre office block were held by the National Asset Management Agency, the State's bad bank, and symbolised the contradiction of widespread homelessness in a city with tens of thousands of vacant properties.

Activists and homeless people occupied the premises for twenty-eight days, providing much-needed emergency accommodation for some rough sleepers over Christmas. Their actions were defended in the High Court and generated enormous levels of public support.

In addition to highlighting the issues involved, the Home Sweet Home occupation secured six-month accommodation placements for almost seventy people who were sleeping rough and raised €190,000 from public donations much of which was subsequently donated to homeless organisations and campaigns. Unfortunately, however, the overall numbers of people in emergency accommodation continued to rise, despite *Rebuilding Ireland* meeting its housing targets.

Government claims that social housing waiting lists were falling from 91,600 in September 2016 to 85,799 in September 2017 were undermined by the fact that those on two-year HAP tenancies and four-year RAS leases were not included in the figures despite clearly having a long-term housing need and in the vast majority of cases a stated preference for standard Council housing.[104] When RAS and HAP tenants were included in the overall social housing need number, the first year of *Rebuilding Ireland* actually witnessed an increase from approximately 128,000 households in 2016 to 132,000 in 2017.[105]

Unsurprisingly not a single affordable home to rent or buy was delivered through any Department of Housing scheme in the first year of *Rebuilding Ireland*. Indeed, house prices and rents continued to spiral upwards.

According to the Daft.ie quarterly price reports, house prices rose by 8.5 percent in 2015 and 8 percent in 2016.[106] By June 2017 they had increased again by 8.8 percent. However, the really dramatic increases were in the urban centres with Dublin City experiencing an 18 percent price hike in the year Simon Coveney was Minister for Housing, while in his own constituency of Cork prices had jumped by 11 percent in the county and 9 percent in the city.[107]

Rents were rising at an even more dramatic pace. According to the Residential Tenancies Board Quarterly Rent Index 2015 had seen annual rent increases of 8 percent in Dublin, 11 percent in the commuter belt counties and 6 percent across the rest of the State.[108] In 2016 rents increased in the State by 8 percent to a standard average of €986 per month.[109] However, rents in most urban centres such as Cork, Galway and the commuter belt had breached €1,000 while in Dublin City the range was from €1,100 in places like Swords to €2,000 in Stillorgan.[110]

The Government response to the growing affordability crisis was twofold, focusing on assisting first-time buyers and restraining rising rents.

The Minister for Finance Michael Noonan had announced a tax relief for first-time buyers in advance of the launch of *Rebuilding Ireland*. The Help to Buy Scheme would allow first-time buyers to reclaim 5 percent of the purchase price of a home up to the value of €400,000 from their future tax liabilities.

Critics of the scheme said it would drive house price inflation and was focused on assisting people to buy overpriced homes rather than providing housing at a lower price. In April 2017 the Governor of the Central Bank Philip Lane said that 'of course' the scheme would add to house price inflation. A report from MyHome.ie and Davy Group three months later said that the scheme had a 'significant impact on the property market'.[111]

In December 2016 the Minister for Housing, Simon Coveney, introduced a series of amendments to the Residential Tenancies Act at a very late stage in the passage through the Dáil of the Planning and Development (Housing) and Residential Tenancies Amendment Bill. The proposal was to introduce Rent Pressure Zones within which rent increases would be capped at 4 percent annually. The criteria for these Zones was four consecutive quarterly rent increases of more than 7 percent with the most recent quarter to be above the statewide average. The 4 percent cap would apply to all existing and new tenancies within the Zone but properties not leased in the previous two years, including new builds and properties that had been 'substantially refurbished', were excluded.

The cumulative cost of the 4 percent if applied each year over three years as allowed by the legislation would amount to a 12.5 percent rent increase, costing an average renter in Dublin a total of €4,500 and an average renter in Cork €3,200.

During the Dáil debate on the amendments on 14 December opposition spokespersons noticed significant drafting errors which would have allowed rent increases of 8 percent, demonstrating the rushed nature of the legislation.[112] Amid scenes of confusion the parliament had to be suspended, the Minister and officials sat in emergency session overnight and revised amendments were presented to opposition spokespersons the following morning.

Despite strong opposition for some parties who objected to the 12.5 percent increase over three years, the exemptions for various property types and the exclusion of many high rent areas due to the high threshold for entry, the amendments passed with the support of Fianna Fáil.

However, rents continued to rise with the RTB index noting a 6 percent annual increase by mid-2017 and a 6.4 percent increase by the end of the year. The average monthly rent across the State increased during the course of the year from €986 in Quarter 4 2016 to €1,054 in Quarter 4 2017, while in Dublin the average rents increased from €1,422 to €1,511 during the same period.

While both the Government and the RTB claimed that the Rent Pressure Zones (RPZ) were slowing the rate of rental inflation this was little comfort to renters who were paying between €800 and €1,050 extra in rent at the end of 2017. Increasingly a two-tier rental market was emerging with long-term secure tenants paying lower rents as their landlords observed the RPZ rules while tenants in new properties to the market and those outside the RPZs faced rent hikes significantly in excess of the 4 percent.

Minister Coveney was also experiencing delays in the delivery of homes targeting homeless families according to the 3rd Quarterly Progress Report on *Rebuilding Ireland* published on 31 May 2017. The €70 million fund for Housing Agency acquisitions was proving to be slow and bureaucratic with no purchases at the time of the report. His Rapid Build Programme was significantly behind schedule having delivered just twenty-two social homes in the first twelve months and coming in at a cost higher than standard social housing construction. Meanwhile no additional Housing First tenancies had been put in place at the end of the first quarter.[113]

Spiralling rents and glacial levels of social housing output led to an ever rising level of housing need and homelessness. Against this backdrop it was hardly surprising that Minister Coveney failed to meet his first major self-imposed deadline. *Rebuilding Ireland* promised to end the use of hotel and BnB accommodation for homeless families in all but the most urgent situations by June 2017. The strength of this Commitment at the launch of *Rebuilding Ireland* in July 2016 led the *Irish Examiner* to headline their coverage on the following day with 'Coveney bets his career on promise to end homelessness'. Their journalist Juno McEnroe reported that, 'A key pledge, to be monitored closely, was the promise to end use of hotels and B&Bs for the homeless in the next year.'[114]

In March 2017 there were 1,256 families in emergency accommodation of which 871 were in commercial hotels and BnBs, the highest number to date. By June the number of homeless families had increased to 1,365 and despite a significant level of expenditure in the provision of new purpose refurbished family HUBs there were still 695 families in accommodation. The Minister had missed his target.

However, as this significant *Rebuilding Ireland* target date approached Minister Coveney was absorbed in a battle for the leadership of his party, and ultimately Taoiseach, which he lost to colleague and Minister for Social Protection Leo Varadkar on 2 June. Within a fortnight he was appointed Tánaiste and Minister for Foreign Affairs.

During the Dáil debate on 14 June, during which his new appointment was announced, I made the following observation:

Simon Coveney has been Minister for Housing for twelve months. Never has a Minister promised so much and delivered so little. In the initial months as Minister he raised people's hopes and expectations. In the end however his legacy in housing is little more than a string of press launches and dodgy statistics. Unfortunately after a year in office the housing and homeless crisis is worse than ever.

Homelessness has increased, as has the cost of renting and buying a home. Meanwhile social housing delivery continues at a snail's pace while the number of people at risk of homelessness continues to rise. Thanks to Minister Coveney the housing crisis is worse today than when he took office.

Minister Coveney's move to Foreign Affairs is a slap in the face to the homeless families he vowed to help. He is turning his back on the people he promised to help including those languishing on social housing waiting lists, those at risk of homelessness or losing their home, those struggling with excessive rents or priced out of the first time buyers market.[115]

His replacement, former Minister of State in the Department of Finance Eoghan Murphy, was not known for his interest in housing policy. A close ally of the new Taoiseach, he had raised the issue of housing just twenty-five times in his six years in the Dáil, of homelessness five times, social housing four times and the private rental sector just once. Whether he could do a better job than his predecessor, given the limited policy tools and investment levels at his disposal, was an open question.

Minister Murphy's Record – June 2017 to December 2018

On his appointment of Eoghan Murphy as Minister for Housing, incoming Taoiseach Leo Varadkar announced that his colleague would undertake a review of *Rebuilding Ireland* with a specific focus on 'what additional measures may be required, including consideration of a greater quantum of social housing build, a vacant home tax and measures to encourage landlords to remain in or enter the rental market'.[116]

Opposition politicians, non-governmental organisations, homeless service providers and others all made submissions to the Department of Housing in the hope of influencing the review. However, no document was ever published. Instead the Minister engaged in a rolling series of announcements, primarily of legislation he intended to publish and policy changes he hoped to make. By October he had made sixty-four separate policy announcements. Nevertheless, on closer inspection many of these were re-announcements of future intentions rather than actual actions.

What did not emerge from this rolling review of *Rebuilding Ireland* was a vacant homes tax (the proposal was quietly dropped in advance of Budget 2019) or measures to encourage landlords to remain in or enter the market (since January 2017 more than 9,000 properties were withdrawn from the rental market). While he did announce an increase in the level of new build social housing, the overall number for 2018 would remain unchanged as the targets for acquisitions were lowered.

He did secure funding for 3,000 additional social houses, announced in October 2017 as part of Budget

2018. However, the funding would not be for that year but would be delivered from 2019 through to 2021 bringing the total number of social houses owned by Local Authorities and Approved Housing Bodies to be delivered during the term of *Rebuilding Ireland* to 40,000.

While the various delivery streams for social housing were on or above target for 2017, progress, particularly with new build and leasing, struggled significantly the following year. Figures released by the Department for Housing in December 2018 showed that as of the end of quarter 3 only 23 percent of the 4,969 Council and Approved Housing Body new builds had been completed. When challenged on the shortfall at the Oireachtas Housing Committee that month the Minister said he was confident that the target would be reached when the final year's figures were in.

The revised targets for 2018 did not only include an increase in builds and a reduction in acquisitions, but also a significant increase in the target for long-term leased units. However, as of the end of September just 476 of the 2,000 promised units had materialised. To make up the shortfall the Government had approved an increase in the number of units to be acquired by Councils and Approved Housing Bodies which brought in 1,661 homes, significantly above the target of 900.

Nevertheless, the overall output for social housing delivery was less than 50 percent of the target, leaving a significant amount of catching up to do in the final quarter of the year. No such difficulties were being experienced with RAS and HAP, both of which were slightly ahead of target with 14,275 new tenancies created in the first nine months, representing 79 percent of their target for the year.

There was also a significant setback when first the Central Statistics Office in December 2017 and then Eurostat in March 2018 reclassified Approved Housing Bodies as part of the general Government sector.[117] The immediate impact of the announcement was for all historic and future borrowing and spending by the not-for-profit sector to go on the Government's balance sheet. Part of the rationale for giving the sector an enhanced role in social housing delivery since 1991 was that their private borrowings and spending were not included in the Government estimates.

While the decision had no impact on the 2018 delivery targets, Housing Associations expressed a concern than if the decision was not reversed it could impact on their ability to deliver on future targets as their borrowing would be constrained, or their ability to spend limited, as they would be more impacted by the politics of the annual Government budget cycle.

In addition to the slow pace of social housing construction there were also ongoing delays with the three funding streams for getting vacant homes back into stock. As of January 2019 just 250 of the vacant units had been brought into use via the Buy and Renew Scheme and 48 units via the Repair and Lease scheme.[118] Both of these figures were significantly lower than the original targets of 3,500 and 500 respectively.[119]

The record of the Housing Agency fund was no better with just 531 homes bought from banks and funds by the start of January 2019 despite over 3,967 properties having been offered to the Agency by banks and funds since 2016. As the properties were then sold on to Approved Housing Bodies before tenanting, an even lower number were actually occupied at the end of 2019 with just 181 units acquired by the sector.[120]

The much-delayed publication of the Government's *Vacant Homes Strategy* took place in July a full year after

Minister Murphy had taken office. Despite the fact that his predecessor had completed the plan before leaving office and its initial delay was understood to be to facilitate the consideration of a vacant property tax, the document contained no targets or extra funding commitments.[121]

While the Central Statistics Office 2016 census estimate of 183,000 vacant homes had been reduced downwards by An Post and GeoDirectories to 90,000 many observers still believed that there was significant 'low hanging fruit' that could be accessed at a lower cost than new build or acquisition for social and affordable use.

There was also a growing concern from opposition politicians that the programme for returning long-term vacant Council properties, known as voids, back into active use was also being used for refurbishment of casual vacancies within the Council stock. This was more than just a statistical question as returned voids represented a real addition to the social housing stock whereas casual relets did not.

The void programme was introduced by Minister for Environment Alan Kelly in 2014 and targeted long-term vacant properties with additional grant funding to Local Authorities to bring them back into stock. At that time, according to the National Oversight and Audit Commission, there were believed to be up to 4,000 such properties across the State. However, in January 2018 Minister Eoghan Murphy claimed that over four years 9,227 voids had been brought back into use, including 1,757 in 2017 alone.[122]

His claim was significantly undermined by Director of Housing for Dublin City Council Brendan Kenny during an Oireachtas Housing Committee meeting on the 26 September of that year. When asked how many of the 543 units from Dublin City that were included in the Minister's voids figures for 2017 were in fact voids, he said 'there were no long term voids'.[123]

Despite all of this, Minister Murphy continued to claim that progress was being made both on the social housing front as within the private sector, pointing out increased planning applications and house completions. However, both housing need and homelessness continued to increase.

The combined Council list, HAP and RAS list figure as of September 2018 was approximately 130,917 households, down less than 2,000 from the previous year's figures despite 4,500 new social homes coming on stream in 2017 and almost 3,400 in the first third of 2018 not to mention up to 3,000 allocations through casual vacancies annually. The low level of social housing delivery could not even keep pace with the level of new need.

On the homeless front things were continuing to get worse. In June 2017 when Murphy took office there were 5,046 adults and 2,895 children officially recognised by his Department as homeless. In January 2019, the latest month for which figures are available, the number of homeless adults had increased by 26 percent to 6,363 and the number of children increased by 25 percent to 3,624. The overall increase in family homeless based on the Department of Housing's official figures was 18 percent from 1,365 in June 2017 to 1,614 in January 2019.[124]

A new phenomenon of pensioner homeless was also evident from the figures with a rise of 39 percent between June 2017 and January 2019. Despite the significant investment in new family-specific homeless HUB accommodation the number of families in commercial hotels and BnBs had also increased.

However, the real level of homelessness was significantly higher than what the official figures from the

Department of Housing suggested. This was in part due to the decision to exclude a number of categories of people from the figures when the methodology was first agreed in 2014. However, more controversially, Minister Murphy unilaterally removed a further 1,609 adults and children from his own Department's reporting during the course of 2018.

The Department of Housing's monthly report originated from a data subgroup of the Homelessness Consultative Forum, a body bringing together Government, NGOs and academics, to develop homeless policy. In 2014 it recommended that all adults and children in Department of Housing (then the Department of Environment) funded emergency and temporary accommodation would be included. Rough sleepers, those in hostels not funded by Government and sofa surfers would not be included.

In 2015 as a result of the transfer of funding for domestic violence shelters to the newly established Department of Children and Family Affairs, this category of homeless households was removed from the Department of Housing's figures.

Thus since 2014 there has been a broadly agreed metric, published monthly, that allowed Government, opposition politicians, service providers and academics to track the levels of homelessness in the State. The methodology wasn't perfect, but it was agreed and understood by all parties.

In a statement accompanying the release of the March homeless figures Minister Murphy said that 'at least 600 individuals have been identified as having been categorised as homeless and in emergency accommodation when they are not'. The Minister went on to state that some of these people have been removed from the official figures and that the Councils were working to gauge the extent of the problem. In total 253 adults and 318 children were removed from the figures.

When the April figures were released at the end of May a further 294 people including 173 children were removed from the figures again on the basis of alleged mis-categorisation by Local Authorities. Then on 27 September the Minister confirmed, under questioning from members of the Oireachtas Housing Committee, that an additional 741 people had been removed from the official figures over the past few months.

In total 1,609 adults and children had been removed from the Department of Housing's homeless figures. A Departmental report published on the same day as the Committee hearing justified the decision saying it had been done in agreement with the Local Authorities as the families were not in emergency accommodation but 'own door accommodation'.

However Local Authority officials, voluntary service providers and academics involved in designing the original methodology all disagreed.

Brendan Kenny, Director of Housing with Dublin City Council, speaking on RTÉ's *Morning Ireland* on 31 May on the re-categorisation of these families said that, 'There's no tenancy agreement, they're still homeless, they're on the homeless list, and they have homeless priority'.

During a special Oireachtas Housing Committee hearing on the issue in November Eileen Gleeson, the Director of the Dublin Regional Homeless Executive, when asked if the families were still homeless at the time of being removed from the monthly report, said, 'Yes I would consider that they are still homeless, because they are accessing homeless services.'[125]

At the same hearing Professor Eoin O'Sullivan from Trinity College Dublin and a member of the original data subgroup in 2014 described the families as 'homeless according to the original definition, that is, being section 10 funded and being a licensee. Whether it is own-door accommodation or a hub does not matter.'[126]

In written submissions to the Committee, leading homeless charities also criticised the removal of the families. The Simon Communities said the re-categorisation is 'a cause for concern' and 'has created confusion and caused a range of problems'. Focus Ireland have said that the rationale for the removal was unclear feeding the 'suspicion that the underlying motive was to produce a lower total figure'.

In total 625 adults and 981 children were removed from the homeless figures by the Minister since the start of the year. While at the time of writing some families have moved on to secure tenancies the majority are still homeless and living in temporary accommodation.

During an Oireachtas Housing Committee meeting on 17 May 2018 the Minister sought to defend his decision by making a distinction between families in commercial hotels and BnBs on the one hand on those in properties owned by Local Authorities or leased from the private sector. In response I argued that

> Perhaps I am seeing a Minister who does not understand the difference between a tenancy and a temporary emergency accommodation arrangement. If he does not understand that fundamental difference, then my opinion is that he is not competent to hold the job he is in because it is such a basic definition in homeless services. Alternatively, he does understand the difference. He knows very well the difference between a tenancy and a temporary licence agreement, but he is

still allowing hundreds of families to be removed from the figures. If that is the case, then I have to say, and it gives me no pleasure to say this, he is not fit to hold the office he holds. The Minister absolutely cannot remove families from homeless figures when they are in emergency accommodation without tenancies.[127]

When all of these people – re-categorised families, rough sleepers, women and children in domestic violence shelters, adults and children in emergency accommodation without Government funding and former asylum seekers who have secured their legal right to remain but due to the housing crisis are forced to use Direct Provision as emergency accommodation – are taken into account, the real level of homelessness at the end of 2018 would be closer to 13,000 people, and that is before we start to consider the issue of hidden homelessness.

On the affordability front Minister Murphy was also in trouble. Since taking office house prices and rents continued to rise. According to Daft.ie house prices rose by 8.8 percent in 2017 and a further 5.5 percent in 2018. The average price of a house was now €254,000 and from €300,000 to €591,000 in Dublin depending on the Local Authority area.[128] Rents at the end of 2017 were up on average 6 percent with the standardised average rent according to the Residential Tenancies Board at €1,054. By the end of the third quarter of 2018 new rents were up a further 7.5 percent with a statewide average of €1,208.[129]

To address the growing affordability crisis Minister Murphy launched a series of measures in January 2018. In addition to a re-announcement of the cost rental pilot promised in *Rebuilding Ireland* the package included a revised Local Authority first-time buyers' mortgage for those unable to access bank credit but with a lower interest rate and a commitment to a new affordable housing scheme in which the State would take an equity stake in the house purchase. Details on the latter were sketchy; however, an initial fund of €25 million was earmarked for the scheme along with €200 million for the Council loan.

Take up of the new Council mortgage was low with just 200 drawdowns by September 2018. A total of 2,222 applications had been deemed eligible with approval granted for 1,134.[130] Applications for funding for Local Authorities to deliver the affordable housing scheme were opened in July and the funding extended to €100 million in Budget 2019. However, at the time of writing no projects have commenced and it is unlikely that any properties will be delivered until 2020 at the earliest. Meanwhile the long-promised cost rental pilot will only commence construction in early 2019 with tenanting expected the following year. A number of other cost rental projects are at early stages in Dublin and Cork City but delivery is not expected for some years.

Meanwhile in June at a hearing of the Oireachtas Housing Committee a senior Department Official admitted that the Local Infrastructure Housing Activation Fund may not deliver affordability in all projects. Indeed, when the final details of the first round of contracts were published it was clear that the vast majority of private developments in receipt of the infrastructure fund would be selling houses above 2017 open market prices, thus well beyond the reach of modest and above average income households.

Affordability was also a growing issue for students. The Department of Education had published its *Student Accommodation Strategy* in May 2018 which identified a shortfall of some 24,000 units of student accommodation in the system. While committing to facilitate public and private provision of an additional 21,000 places by 2024 the strategy itself admitted that when increased student numbers are taken into account there will still be a shortfall of 20,000 beds in that year.

Meanwhile students in Dublin City and Galway City universities were hit with rent increases of between 18 percent and 30 percent leading to significant protests in March and April at Shanowen Court in North County Dublin and Cúirt an Coiribe in Galway City. The Student Unions at both campuses supported by the Union of Students in Ireland demanded that student-specific accommodation be given the full protection of the Residential Tenancies Act including the cover of Rent Pressure Zones, limiting rent increases to 4 percent.

While student-specific accommodation provided by universities was explicitly excluded from these protections the Residential Tenancies Board argued that private student-specific accommodation was covered.[131] However, in April both Sinn Féin and Fianna Fáil published legislation to remove all doubt by explicitly including all student-specific accommodation within the Act.

The Sinn Féin Bill was passed without opposition from the Government on 2 May and Minister Murphy subsequently gave a commitment to address the issue in his own forthcoming Residential Tenancies Amendment Bill 2018, the passage of which commenced in January 2019.

Alongside the affordability of rental accommodation, significant problems with the standards in the private rental sector were exposed in an *RTÉ Investigates* documentary 'Nightmare to Let', broadcast at the start of November 2017. The programme exposed landlords packing tenants into unsafe and insanitary conditions, where the risk of fire and death was immediately apparent. The programme once again highlighted the low level of inspections of rental properties in many Local Authorities and the even lower level of enforcement and sanction.

Threshold advocated strongly for an NCT-style system of certification, managed by Local Authorities and mandatory for all rental properties. A Sinn Féin Private Members Motion in line with the Threshold proposals was tabled and passed in the Dáil shortly after the RTÉ documentary was broadcast. However, despite a commitment to review the law on sanctions and overcrowding no action has been taken by the Minister a year on. His one commitment has been to reach a 25 percent inspection rate for all rental properties by 2021 and to progressively increase funding to Councils year on year to achieve this.

On a more positive note the Minister committed to increase the powers of the Residential Tenancies Board to police and enforce the rent review legislation, allowing the Board to initiate their own investigations and impose sanctions. The legislation is also to include a public rent register to encourage greater price transparency in the market. An initial timeline of having the legislation completed by Winter 2018 was not met. At the time of writing the Bill is making its way through the Oireachtas. However, following the intervention of the Attorney General Séamus Woulfe, whose orthodox views on the issue of administrative justice are well known, the power of the RTB to apply sanctions is to be constrained by the courts which if not removed from the Bill will severely limit the effectiveness of the new powers.

Similar delays were experienced in the legislation dealing with the regulation of the short-term letting sector. Following calls from opposition politicians in October 2016 the then Minister for Housing Simon Coveney established a Departmental working group following February to examine the issue. In December 2017 the Oireachtas Housing Committee published a detailed report calling for regulations for the sector including a planning permission requirement for those letting out their own home for more than ninety nights or those renting out non-primary dwellings on a commercial basis.

In September 2018 the Minister announced his plans which were broadly in line with the Oireachtas Housing Committee's proposals and then published the General Scheme of the Bill in November. However, at the time of writing neither the regulations nor legislation have been published and they will not come into effect until mid-2019 at the earliest.

The other key feature of Minister Murphy's tenure to date has been changes to regulations governing apartment buildings. A report by the Institute of Chartered Surveyors in 2018 demonstrated that there was a significant viability and affordability gap in apartment construction, particularly in Dublin. Their findings were confirmed by a Department of Housing report into residential development costs published in April. In response the Minister relaxed the regulations on apartment sizes, dual aspect design and car parking requirements and introduced regulations overriding the height restrictions on apartment developments in a number of Local Authorities.

While both moves may make apartments more financially viable for some developers, on the basis of the figures detailed in both the Institute of Chartered Surveyors and Department of Housing reports neither move is likely to have any meaningful impact on affordability.

The Minister appeared less interested in tackling the legacy of bad apartment development from the Celtic Tiger era. In January 2018 the Oireachtas Housing Committee published a detailed report titled *Safe as Houses? A Report on Building Standards, Building Control and Consumer Protection*. Among its recommendations was a redress scheme to assist those who had bought properties during the boom only to subsequently learn of significant structural problems relating to fire safety and water ingress.

Despite the issue being raised by a number of opposition deputies on foot of the report alongside significant lobbying for hundreds of affected apartment owners across the country, no such scheme was introduced in Budget 2019. The Government also failed to implement other key recommendations from the report such as mandatory latent defect insurance or legal reform of warranties and statutes of limitation.

In September, to much fanfare, the Government launched an initiative that they claimed would be a game changer in the housing system. Building on key recommendations in a number of National Economic and Social Council reports from 2004 to 2017 on the issue of active land management, the Taoiseach, Minister for Finance and Minister for Housing announced the Land Development Agency (LDA). Speaking at its unveiling Leo Varadkar said:

> The Land Development Agency, with capital of €1.25 billion behind it, is a step change in the Government's involvement in the housing market. We are going to build new homes and lots of them. That includes social housing, affordable housing, private housing and cost rental housing on both publicly and privately owned land.[132]

There was widespread approval for the land management functions of the LDA, taking a long-term strategic view of all of the State's land holdings including those of semi-State companies, and having the power and funds to move land to greater strategic uses such as residential development.

However, the decision to develop the land via public-private joint venture partnerships and restrict the social housing allocation on any given site to just 10 percent and the affordable housing allocation to 30 percent was widely criticised. At a time of growing need for social and affordable housing allowing 60 percent of its major land holdings to be used for over-valued open market price housing hardly seemed the strategically or indeed morally correct thing to do.

Throughout the course of 2018 there was a growing public perception that Eoghan Murphy was out of his depth and unable to get a grip on the housing crisis. Newspaper journalists and radio broadcasters were quoting anonymous Fine Gael back benchers and Ministerial colleagues who were expressing dissatisfaction with his failure to deliver. Hugh O'Connell writing in the *Sunday Business Post* in November quoted sources close to Government who claimed that the Taoiseach was getting 'frustrated' with his Minister's handling of the housing portfolio.[133] In January, the *Irish Mail on Sunday* ran the following headline on their front page, 'Varadkar "Losing Faith in Housing Minister"'.[134] The two-page spread quoted anonymous Cabinet colleagues saying the Taoiseach was 'exasperated' with Murphy's failure to get to grips with the housing crisis and that the once close relationship between the two has been replaced by a 'coldness between them'.[135]

There were also growing protests on the street. In April 8,000 people marched in Dublin in a demonstration organised by the Housing and Homeless Coalition, supported by NGOs, grass roots housing action groups, trade unions and opposition political parties. In August a new direct action group, Take Back the City, started a series of occupations of derelict buildings in Dublin's city centre to highlight the scandal of vacant housing at a time of huge housing need. Following a violent eviction from an occupation in North Fredrick Street an impromptu protest attracted thousands in early September.

Later that month Sinn Féin tabled a motion of no confidence in the Housing Minister, calling for both a change of personnel and a change of policy. Proposing the motion at the start of the debate I said:

> When Deputy Eoghan Murphy was appointed Minister for Housing, Planning and Local Government fifteen months ago I said I wanted him to succeed. I told the House that if he implemented the right policies I would commend him, but I also said I would hold him to account if he pursued the wrong options. Fifteen months later, it is clear that both Deputy Eoghan Murphy, as Minister, and his housing policy, *Rebuilding Ireland*, have failed ... Passing this motion tonight would send a clear signal to the Government that its housing policy must change. It would ensure that budget 2019 would be a housing budget. It could be a turning point in our housing and homelessness crisis. However, if Fianna Fáil and Fine Gael will not listen to the Opposition they will have to listen to the people.[136]

In his defence the Housing Minister argued that Fine Gael did not create the housing crisis, that he would not be 'hounded out of office' and that *Rebuilding Ireland* 'was working'. He told the Dáil that

> More new homes will be provided this year than in any year in the past decade. Over 20,000 new places to live in will be delivered and still we have more to do. My job as Minister is to get it done but I will not be distracted by populist nonsense that contributes nothing to the challenges that we face.[137]

Despite strong criticism of the Government's failure to deliver on the housing front from Fianna Fáil's new housing spokesperson Darragh O'Brien his party abstained on the final vote, ensuring that both Minister Murphy and *Rebuilding Ireland* would remain in situ. Forty-nine Deputies voted for the motion of no confidence; fifty-nine voted against and twenty-nine abstained. Minister Murphy survived but only 43 percent of the Dáil had clear confidence in him.

The following week brought the largest housing demonstration to date, this time to the front gates of the Dáil. A new coalition, Raise the Roof, led by the Irish Congress of Trade Unions (ICTU) and supported by the Housing and Homeless Coalition, the National Women's Council of Ireland, the Union of Students in Ireland and a number of leading homeless charities assembled to demand a change of policy from Government.

Speaking at the launch of the initiative two weeks earlier, Congress President Sheila Nunan said:

> This crisis is an issue for everyone. It is now almost impossible for workers, young families and students to secure decent, affordable accommodation and this

has put intolerable pressure on living standards across all sectors. We need to see a dramatic increase in the supply of quality, affordable public housing. Housing is a human right and should not be the plaything of speculators.[138]

The press conference also heard from veteran homeless campaigner Fr Peter McVerry who told the assembled media:

When will the emperor finally realise that he has no clothes? Homeless figures are up, house prices are up and the fact that government policy has failed is staring us all in the face. The old refrain from government that 'we just need more time' just does not wash anymore. We need to see a dramatic change in policy to resolve this worsening crisis.[139]

Orla O'Connor of the National Women's Council also highlighted the gendered nature of the crisis arguing that

The crisis is clearly a woman's issue, with our rate of female homelessness now double that of other European countries. More than 60% of homeless families are lone parent families, the majority lone mothers. The shocking rates of women and child homelessness are a result of the dramatic increase in families forced from their homes due to rising rents, the majority of whom are women-headed lone parent families.[140]

The mobilisation of 15,000 people coincided with a cross-party opposition motion that was being debated in the chamber, signed by forty-nine Deputies. The motion was based on an ICTU Charter launched earlier in the year and called on the Government to

- Declare the housing and homeless crisis an emergency
- Dramatically increase the supply of social and affordable (including cost rental) housing by increasing capital spending on housing to €2.3bn in budget 2019; increase Part V requirements to 20 percent in standard developments and 30 percent in Strategic Development Zones; prioritise the delivery of public housing on public land; and aggressively target the return of vacant houses to active use
- Reduce the flow of adults and children into homelessness with the introduction of emergency legislation to make it illegal for landlords, banks and investment funds to evict tenants and homeowners in mortgage distress into homelessness; provide real security of tenure and real rent certainty by linking rent reviews to an index such as the CPI and introducing measures to reduce the cost of rent; introduce a target for ending long-term homelessness and the need to sleep rough
- Hold a referendum to enshrine the right to housing in the Constitution.

Significantly, though not signatories to the motion, Fianna Fáil supported it in the final vote. Its passing was a symbolic but nonetheless significant defeat for the Government. Fianna Fáil abstained in the following week's Budget announcement, which fell far short of the previous week's motion. Nevertheless, the Raise the Roof initiative set a new bar in the public debate on the housing crisis.

The Housing and Homeless Coalition held another demonstration in Dublin on 1 December, the fourth anniversary of the tragic death of Jonathan Corrie in 2014, a rough sleeper who died late in the night on the steps of a building opposite the parliament. Over 10,000 people attended the rally demanding greater investment in public housing and an end to the homeless crisis.

Both Raise the Roof and its constituent members gave a clear commitment that 2019 would see bigger and more intense campaigning and mobilisation on the housing issue until the Government and Fianna Fáil listened and changed policy direction. Campaigners were also clear that if the necessary policy and investment changes weren't made then it would focus on changing the Government instead.

Eoghan Murphy's future as Minister for Housing is uncertain. At the end of 2018 Leo Varadkar indicated considering a cabinet reshuffle in mid-2019. However, whatever about the individual holding Ministerial office, on the basis of Budget 2019 *Rebuilding Ireland* will remain Government housing policy until such time as the public, whether on the streets or in the ballot box, force a change of direction and an increase in investment commensurate with the level of social and affordable housing need.

Conclusion

The 1980s and 1990s brought about a transformation in the Southern Irish housing system. Recession from the late 1980s led Government to withdraw from the direct financing of both social and owner-occupied housing. While the change didn't happen overnight, by the mid-1990s Government involvement in housing provision had returned to levels not seen since the 1920s.

The two most significant impacts on the overall functioning of the housing system was the increasing residualisation of social housing both in terms of the size of the sector and the socio-economic profile of its tenants and the financialisation of the private housing sector, including both owner-occupation and private rental.

A Plan for Social Housing, by ending large-scale investment in Council-led housing developments, drove a self-fulfilling prophesy in which new social housing conformed to the misplaced stereotypes that policy makers and politicians had of Council housing pre the 1970s.

The plan, in its failure to directly meet social housing need via Councils and Approved Housing Bodies, also had the unintended consequences of diverting social housing applicants into the private rental sector. Rent subsidies went from being an accidental social housing support in the 1990s through Rent Supplement to an officially defined long-term housing support with RAS from 2004 and then HAP from 2014.

Significantly, in the twenty-five years from *A Plan for Social Housing* to *Rebuilding Ireland* the reliance on subsidised private rental tenancies to meet social housing need increased to such an extent that it has become the largest component of the Government housing strategy.

The significance of this is threefold. Firstly, as Joe Finnerty and Cathal O'Connell rightly point out, the shift to short-term private sector tenancies represents a 'casualisation' of social housing.[141] Tenancies are shorter and subject to the interests of the landlord and the vagaries of the market, making long-term planning for tenants more difficult. This not only negatively affects the household but undermines longer-term neighbourhood stability as subsidised rental tenants find it more difficult to become embedded in their communities.

Secondly, the cost to the State, while lower on an annual basis, is significantly more expensive in the long term as highlighted by the Department of Public Expenditure and Reform *Analysis of Current Expenditure on Housing Supports* in 2017.[142] The combined cost for Rent Supplement, RAS, HAP and private sector SHCEP was €640 million in 2018 and there is no reason to believe it won't pass the €1 billion mark in 2021 if the *Rebuilding Ireland* targets are met.

Thirdly, the reliance on the private sector and rental sector to meet social housing need has a significant impact on supply and cost for non-social housing tenants seeking to rent. Almost a third of all rental tenancies are subsidised social housing tenants (45,000 HAP, 36,000 Rent Supplement, 19,000 RAS, 5,440 private SHCEP). Not only do State subsidies create an artificial floor on rents but non-social renters, especially those on low incomes, are crowded out or forced to pay unaffordable rents.

While the State continues to have a significant role in social housing financing and regulation, it is no longer the central agent in the delivery of public housing. By 2018 this change has become completely embedded at the very core of the policy consensus that governs the policies of both Fianna Fáil and Fine Gael.

In the private sector the withdrawal of the State as a key financier of owner-occupation has had an equally profound impact. Domestic financial liberalisation in the 1980s and European Union liberalisation in the 1990s has transformed the nature of house financing. The direct consequence has been the increasing commodification and financialisation of the private housing market.

Between the late 1980s and 2018 the decision to invest in building or buying a house was informed as much by considerations of speculative gain as it was home building. As ever expanding financial providers sought out ever more lucrative markets a toxic housing-finance feedback cycle was put in motion, driving up prices and forcing decisions on housing to be made not according to public need or proper planning but on the basis of bottom line return.

This cycle lay at the heart of the rise of the Celtic Tiger from 1996 and the global Great Recession from 2008. It drove up house prices and rents, and fuelled an affordability crisis that in turn accelerated the social housing and homelessness crises in the decade after the recession.

While post-crash bank caution and sensible macro-prudential mortgage lending regulations by the Central Bank have constrained mortgage credit for individual households it would be wrong to think that the Celtic Tiger era housing-finance feedback cycle is gone. Rather the risks to our housing system from the financial sector have simply moved from household lending to a host of investment vehicles.

Writing in *The Irish Times* in June 2018, the economist and global justice campaigner Ann Pettifor argued that

> To understand Ireland's housing crisis we need to lift our eyes from the micro- to the global macro-economy.
>
> To follow 'the Great Wall of Money' – $453 billion (€390 billion) – aimed at global markets in real estate.
>
> Ireland is just one country whose finite and fixed stock of land and property is massively inflated by this

onslaught of unregulated capital. Dublin as a major international financial centre attracted large volumes of unregulated, cross-border flows.

Above all, Dublin is host to valuable and scarce assets – property. The global owners of capital are in a frantic search for safe, high-yielding assets in which to park their capital.

At a time when Europe's elites are committed to flawed economic austerity policies, there is a shortage of the very safe public assets preferred by global asset management funds or insurance companies: government debt (bonds or gilts).

As a result, those responsible for investing vast sums aim their billions at property markets which, while not as safe as government bonds, are nevertheless considered safer than other assets.

That explains why, €4.47 billion was invested in Irish commercial property in 2016 with total turnover 21 per cent higher than in the previous year.

House prices have been blasted into the stratosphere, not because of a shortage of supply, but by the excess of a potent propellant – finance.[143]

While the initial focus of this 'propellant' was the distressed commercial assets held by the National Asset Management Agency, it is increasingly focusing its attention on residential developments in the owner-occupier and rental markets. The generous tax incentives introduced by the then Minister for Finance Michael Noonan and his Secretary General John Moran to encourage international finance to invest in Irish Real Estate Investment Trusts, Irish Collective Asset Management Vehicles and Irish Qualifying Investor Funds are playing the same role today as cuts to Stamp Duty and Capital Gains Tax, abolition of Residential Property Tax and Section 23 tax relief for landlords played in the 1990s and 2000s.

More troubling still is the desperate attempts by Government to incentivise this 'Great Wall of Money' into the social housing sector, a sector whose defining characteristic is its non-market not-for-profit nature. The return of Public Private Partnerships and introduction of long-term leasing in the *Social Housing Strategy 2020* which was further advanced by the elevation of Joint Ventures and Enhanced Leasing Scheme in *Rebuilding Ireland* and the Land Development Agency are opening up the last remaining sector of the housing system to commodification and financialisation, the consequences of which, if successful, will be profound.

Thus our housing system today is characterised by two key features – an ever smaller public housing sector catering for the very poor in our society and an increasingly financialised private market seeking out safe short-term secure yields on its investment irrespective of the impact its decisions have on people's ability to access appropriate, secure and affordable accommodation.

This is the consequence of a housing policy consensus which since the *Plan for Social Housing* in 1991 saw the State walk away from what had been its primary responsibility in housing policy during the first half of the twentieth century, namely to guarantee that all people could access secure, appropriate and affordable accommodation. The decisions made by successive Governments from the 1990s to the present have left us with a dysfunctional housing system in which an ever growing number of people are in serious housing need. Politicians in power had other options, they could have made different choices, but instead they brought us to where we are today. The question now is whether we will continue to let them make the same choices or start to put in place a real alternative.

Movement 3

The Return of the State?

Taking a Step Back

The Southern Irish housing system has undergone two periods of development and transformation since the late nineteenth century which have brought us to where we are today. If we are to chart a course for the future that addresses the significant structural problems in that system – that ends the dysfunction forcing people into bad, abnormal and difficult housing situations – and replaces it with a functional system that provides people with appropriate, secure and affordable homes, then we need to fully understand the core of the problem we have to address.

The first phase in the development of our housing system took place from the 1880s to the end of the mid-1980s. It gave the State a progressively greater role in securing people's housing need through subsidising owner-occupation and the provision of public housing. It did this in a way that privileged the first while not completely relegating the second. Through extensive tenant purchase it also allowed those in public housing, who otherwise would never have had the means to own homes, to do so.

This policy of 'asset based welfare' produced a relatively stable housing system that by the 1970s had cleared the slums and provided most working people with homes of a decent standard while protecting the majority of low-income families from the indignities of the unscrupulous private landlord and the vast majority of homeowners from the vagaries of the market.

It is, however, important not to be naïve about that system, as it was not without its problems. Inequalities, particularly for Travellers and those with disabilities, were widespread. Homelessness remained a constant feature. Poor quality building, bad planning, inappropriate relationships between some politicians and developers and inadequate social and economic infrastructure caused problems for tens of thousands of households.

However, the State did take on the responsibility, particularly from the 1940s to the 1970s, of mitigating the risks inherent in the private housing market by playing a strong interventionist role.

The primary weakness of the system was the exceptionally high level of owner-occupation. As long as Government was willing to underwrite much of this through grants, low cost loans, tax reliefs and tenant purchase discounts, the inherent risks went unseen. Nevertheless, when confronted with the fiscal crisis of the State from the late 1970s onwards these risks came into sharp focus.

The second phase of our housing system's development was from the late 1980s to the present. While owner-occupation has fallen somewhat and private rental overtaken social rental, the overall shape of the system in terms of tenure distribution has remained broadly intact. What has changed however is the way in which the system in funded.

Financial liberalisation has removed the safety net provided by Government to private purchasers and social renters in previous decades. This has exposed new generations to the volatility of the market, fuelling repeated affordability crises. Excessive rents, mortgage distress, overcrowding, and delayed household formation are all key features of this increasingly precarious housing system.

Not only have levels of instability increased but so too have levels of inequality in access to housing. This has been compounded by the shrinking of the public housing sector which itself is at further risk from the introduction of ever greater levels of private finance.

Rather than the improved life-cycle 'choice' and 'flexibility' that was promised by the NESC 2005 *Developmental Welfare State* report, the changes to social housing provision – reductions in real social housing output and increases in subsidised tenancies in the private rental sector – has resulted in its opposite. Longer waiting lists, greater insecurity of tenure, ever more complex management arrangements, lower-quality maintenance and growing variance of rights for tenants depending on the social housing provider.

Crucially the excessive level of private ownership – both owner-occupation and private rental – in our housing system makes it more vulnerable to shocks, such as property crashes and recessions, than systems with greater tenure diversity.

Peadar Kirby, in a number of important studies of the development of the Southern Irish State from the 1990s, correctly makes the point that neoliberalism does not involve the withdrawal of the State from all areas of intervention.[1] Rather the State adopts a different kind of interventionist role, withdrawing from the direct provision of universal social and economic services, and increasingly becomes a regulator of market provisions. Both he and Mary Murphy have counterposed the idea of a Competition State to the NESC idea of a Developmental Welfare State as a more appropriate way of understanding the economic and social policies of successive Governments since the 1980s.[2]

The consequences of this neoliberal policy shift are threefold: the emergence of a weak State alongside the rise of market mechanisms to meet social need; rising levels of social and economic inequality as access to key social provisions – such as housing – is determined by ability to pay rather than need; and a more general vulnerability of the economy – and individual households – to systemic shocks such as recession.

While it is broadly accepted that the liberalisation of mortgage finance and the high-risk lending to the domestic mortgage market was a key factor in the Celtic Tiger boom and subsequent recession, there is a misplaced assumption in some quarters today that post-crash reforms have removed the vulnerability to such systemic risks. However, as Ryan-Collins points out, what has actually happened is that the site of potential risk has shifted.

He has argued that the policies of quantitative easing pursued by Central Banks across the world, including the ECB, since 2009 have 'together bought up more than €11 trillion-worth (as of early 2018) of Government bonds and other safe assets from investors, replacing it with zero-interest newly created money'.[3] Rather than being invested in the productive economy, however, this 'wall of liquidity created by QE catalysed a global search for high yielding, but safe assets'.[4] Namely landed property in the world's largest cities.

In the first instance, when some of this 'wall of liquidity' arrived in Ireland, it came looking for distressed commercial assets, such as those held by the National Asset Management Agency. It was received with open arms and generous tax breaks by Government. However, as the market for those assets dried up it has now moved into residential development.

Ryan-Collins traces the recent global trends in which short-term funds are increasingly investing in residential property – both private rental and social housing – not to provide long-term reasonable returns through the provision of secure and affordable accommodation, but to take advantage of short-term market opportunities irrespective of the social or systemic consequences. His conclusions are worrying:

It would appear that rather than addressing the root cause of the financial crisis of 2007–8 in the misallocation of credit to the housing market, in part enabled by securitisation, European authorities have instead focused on how to prop up a bloated and real-estate addicted banking sector by repositioning securitisation as an attractive and safe form of investment … in their efforts to kick-start the economy and revive the banking system post-crisis, governments and central banks have drawn capital markets and a range of other global investors into the housing-finance feedback cycle … This wall of liquidity has been good for the banking system … It has not been good news for citizens of advanced economies who have seen their wages fail to keep pace with rising land and property prices.[5]

There are those who would say, 'this time is different', 'we won't make the same mistakes again' or 'we are not experiencing a housing bubble'. But we heard these arguments in the years before 2008.

In a section on 'anxieties' in the housing system in the 2004 NESC report *Housing in Ireland* this same argument was in evidence. There was clearly a difference of opinion within the Council on the level of risk building up in the housing market in 2004 and whether that risk would lead to a significant downturn in property prices and asset values. The report ultimately erred on the side of optimism and failed to warn strongly enough of the possibility of a hard landing. This time we should err on the side of caution, and embrace the key recommendation of the NESC report, to expand the provision of social and cost rental housing with considerable vigour.

Public housing, whether provided by Government, Approved Housing Bodies, cooperatives or community land trusts not only meets individual housing need but provides a much-needed buffer to the impact of market shocks on the overall housing system. The larger the public housing sector the greater the buffer.

While there are a range of other policy interventions that are required to avoid or limit the impact of future shocks (some of which will be discussed below) the expansion of public housing on a scale not seen in the history of the State is the single most important, both to meet the growing demand for appropriate, secure and affordable housing and to protect our system in a way that policy makers, market operators and politicians failed to do during the Celtic Tiger era.

However, this would require Government policy to become truly tenure neutral, as outlined in the Department of Environment's 2011 *Housing Policy Statement*. But for tenure neutrality to mean anything, Government must not only end its privileging of owner-occupation but it must also ensure through its investment decisions, policies and regulations that public housing and indeed private rental accommodation are available to those for whom these tenures are appropriate. This would require a radical recalibration of existing housing policy along with significant legislative reform and increased public investment.

It would also allow for greater life-cycle 'choice' and 'flexibility' in a way that the housing policies underpinned by the 2005 NESC *Developmental Welfare State* report could never actually achieve.

Today we have a two-tier housing system made up of those with appropriate, secure and affordable homes and a growing number left to the mercy of the market. The lack of an adequate buffer means that when the next crash comes, as it inevitably will, our system will be even less able to cope, imposing significant financial and emotional hardship on those least well served by the current system.

But it doesn't have to be this way. The 2004 National Economic and Social Council's report *Housing in Ireland* pointed part of the way forward when it made the case for an expanded public housing sector to meet social and affordable housing need. However, we need to go even further. It is time to start seeing housing as a right, fundamental to human well-being, and to mobilise the resources of the State to transform our divided housing system into one which meets the needs of the many not just the few.

A Right to Housing

In July 2012 the Fine Gael–Labour Government established a Convention to consider potential changes to the State's

Constitution. Written in 1937 under the stewardship of Fianna Fáil Taoiseach Éamon de Valera and passed following a referendum in the same year, the document broadly reflected the social, economic and cultural values of the time. While Catholic and conservative in much of its emphasis, many commentators have acknowledged that it was more liberal than the ideological consensus prevailing in other Catholic democracies of the time.

Whatever of its origins, in more recent decades there have been growing calls for the text to be comprehensively updated or replaced, to reflect a more modern, liberal and diverse Ireland. The Constitutional Convention, made up of sixty-six citizens selected randomly and thirty-three parliamentarians reflecting the balance within the Oireachtas, was given the job of examining various aspects of the State's fundamental law and to make recommendations to Government for change.

The 9th Plenary of the Convention was held over the weekend of 22–3 February 2014 to consider the issue of Economic, Social and Cultural rights (ESC). The Convention heard from a range of Irish and international advocates and experts on the issues of ESC rights and constitutional law, examined practices in other jurisdictions and listened to a 'for and against' debate with a number of well-known Irish figures.

Following discussion and deliberation, members of the Convention voted on a series of propositions. The central recommendation of the final report was:

> a large majority (85%) of the members favouring changes to the Constitution in order to strengthen the protection of ESC rights. The Convention also recommended that there should be a constitutional

provision that the State would progressively realise ESC rights, subject to maximum available resources, and that this duty would be cognisable by the courts, and that the provision would not diminish the level of protection already afforded in the Constitution.[6]

Forty-three percent of the Convention's members, when asked, wanted to refer the matter elsewhere for further consideration before any action was taken. However, substantial majorities supported inserting the rights to housing, social security, rights for those with disabilities, healthcare and language and cultural rights into the Constitution.

The results of the various ballots make for interesting reading and are worth reproducing in full:

Amendments to the Constitution

	Yes	No	No Opinion
1. In principle, should the Constitution be amended to strengthen the protection of Economic, Social and Cultural rights?	85%	15%	
	Now	Elsewhere	No Opinion
2. In the event that the Convention votes in favour of reform, does the Convention wish to make recommendations now or refer it elsewhere for further consideration of the implications of possible reforms?	56%	43%	1%

3. If the Convention wishes to make recommendations on the issue now, which options are best? (Rank in order of your preference, 1, 2, 3)*

Option 1: Update Article 45 but keep the first paragraph ('... principles of social policy ... for the general guidance of the Oireachtas ... not ... cognisable by any Court')	24%
Option 2: Insert provision along the lines that the State shall <u>endeavour</u> to progressively realise ESC rights, subject to maximum available resources, and that this duty is cognisable by the Courts	16%
Option 3: Insert provision that the State shall progressively realise ESC rights, subject to maximum available resources and that this duty is cognisable by the Courts	59%

4. In the event that the Convention wishes to make recommendations on the issue now, are there specific additional rights that should be enumerated in the Constitution?

	Yes	No	No Opinion
Housing	84%	8%	8%
Social Security	78%	12%	10%
Essential Health Care	87%	6%	7%
Rights for people with disabilities	90%	3%	7%
Linguistic and cultural rights	75%	15%	9%
Rights covered by the International Covenant on ESC rights	80%	10%	10%

During the debate on the merits or otherwise of enshrining such rights in the Constitution, former Progressive

Democratic Government Minister and Senior Counsel
Michael McDowell asked:

> Do we want to devalue politics? Do we trust our
> politicians to deal with our obligations under the UN
> Conventions and the like; to provide the resources that
> are necessary; to make the decisions on the distribution
> of resources? ... In my view it is the essence of the
> integrity of the political process that we stand by it
> however imperfect it has been and that we don't at
> this stage seek to say huge areas of public policy are
> henceforth to be determined by what judge says the
> Constitution says in those areas.[7]

Dr Mary Murphy from the Irish Human Rights and
Equality Commission rejected claims that politics would be
devalued arguing that

> enumerated rights, democratically determined, limit
> judicial activism and clearly demarcate Government's
> policy role. In fact enumerated rights can reinforce the
> separation of power ... [and] give a framework with
> which to manage resource limitations and to protect
> the most vulnerable ... Justiciable economic and social
> rights offer opportunity to restore faith and trust in
> political institutions ...[8]

Despite the overwhelming majority of the Convention
members voting in favour of enshrining Economic, Social
and Cultural rights into the State's Constitution, the report
and its recommendations remained unimplemented during
the lifetime of the Government.

In 2016 the Mercy Law Centre, one of Ireland's
leading housing rights advocacy groups, launched the first

of what would be three reports on the issue of the right to housing. The document highlighted the fact that the right to adequate housing was contained in the Universal Declaration of Human Rights, the International Covenant on Economic and Social Rights and the European Social Charter. They also listed a range of EU member States including Belgium, Finland, Greece, the Netherlands, Portugal, Spain and Sweden who have a constitutional right to housing.

Importantly, the report challenged the mis-perception that a right to housing would entitle everyone to a free home overnight provided by Government, stating clearly that

> A right to housing in the Constitution would not mean the right to a key to a home for all. A Constitutional right to housing would however put in place a basic floor of protection. It would require the State, in its decisions and policies, to reasonably protect the right. It would recognise that a home is central to the dignity and possibility of every person.[9]

The Dáil Housing and Homeless Committee invited the Mercy Law Centre to present the findings of its report on 10 May 2016 and to make the case as to why the right to housing should be in the Committee's final report. Solicitor Maeve Regan outlined the key value of such a right. She told members that

> The right to housing would mean that the courts could look at the State decision or policy and consider whether it was proportionate by reference to the right. It would mean that government and State policies and

actions would have to reasonably protect the right. For example, if the State decided to cut funding for homeless accommodation, the courts could review that ... This is not simply about going to court, as cases are rare. The right to housing would mean that legislation and policy would have to be proofed to ensure they reasonably protect the right, in the same way as they are proofed in regard to other substantive rights. This would ensure that at that early stage a check would be in place to ensure the legislation or policy reasonably protect the right to housing. This would mean that policies on housing and homelessness could not be based on a political whim or simply based on the philosophy of the reigning government. Policy would instead be grounded in the basic obligation to respect the right. In that sense, it would be an enduring protection ...[10]

During the subsequent private sessions of the Committee the constitutional right to housing was just one of only two issues on which agreement could not be reached. While no member of the Committee was against the right in principle, neither Fianna Fáil nor Fine Gael were willing to agree a firm recommendation calling for a referendum.

Instead the Committee agreed a much weaker reaffirmation of the Programme for Government Commitment for the Joint Oireachtas Committee on Housing (separate to the temporary Dáil Housing and Homeless Committee) to consider the matter and 'bring the deliberations in this regard to a conclusion as quickly as possible by bringing a recommendation on the matter to Government'.[11]

However despite insisting on this wording Fine Gael and Fianna Fáil subsequently referred the Report of the

Constitutional Convention dealing with Economic, Social and Cultural Rights to the Oireachtas Finance Committee for consideration. This Committee, rather than the Housing Committee, would now have the responsibility of making a recommendation to the Government.

When proposing the motion to refer on 28 September 2017, Minister for Housing Eoghan Murphy said that the Finance Committee should be cognisant of the 'balance of rights, good governance (including the separation of powers) and resource prioritisation'.[12]

Despite the Constitutional Convention giving the Government a clear mandate to act, the matter was effectively being buried by Government in a Committee which had neither the competence nor the political will to deal with the issue.

Just days earlier a People Before Profit Private Members Bill seeking to hold a referendum to enshrine the right to housing in the Constitution was defeated by a majority of 73 to 37 as Fine Gael and Fianna Fáil voted the proposal down, just as they had done with a similar Bill from Sinn Féin TD Arthur Morgan in 2003.

While the Oireachtas Housing Committee had been stripped of its responsibility to formally make a recommendation to Government on foot of the Constitutional Convention report, it could still discuss the matter and so invited UN Special Rapporteur on the Right to Housing, Leilani Farah, to present to the Committee in June 2018.

Farah expressed concern that the Irish Government had a 'reservation on housing rights provisions in the European Social Charter and [had] yet to ratify the optional protocol to the International Covenant on Economic, Social and Cultural Rights'. Nevertheless, she reminded the Committee that the State still had international legal obligations under the terms of the Millennium Development Goals to ensure 'access for all to adequate, safe and affordable housing and basic services by 2030, which also means ending homelessness within this timeframe'.[13] She strongly argued that

> The best way forward for Ireland to address the housing crisis and meet its international human rights commitments and obligations is to adopt a human rights-based housing strategy or a national action plan that recognises and implements housing as a human right. Why are human rights so essential to housing strategies? Homelessness and grossly inadequate or unaffordable housing are an assault on dignity and life and go to the heart of what triggers, or what should trigger, human rights concern. Human rights violations of this nature demand human rights responses. Human rights demand that governments interact with people who are homeless and inadequately housed as rights holders empowered to engage and be involved in decisions affecting their lives. A rights-based approach clarifies who is accountable to whom: all levels of government are accountable to people, particularly marginalised and vulnerable groups. Human rights incorporate universal norms that bring coherence and co-ordination to multiple areas of law and policy through a common purpose and a shared set of values.[14]

While the Oireachtas Finance Committee has yet to consider the 8th Report of the Constitutional Convention the cross-party housing motion proposed by thirty-eight Deputies on 3 October as part of the Raise the Roof initiative had an explicit call for the holding of a referendum to enshrine the right to housing into the Constitution. Significantly, despite their previous reservations, Fianna Fáil supported the motion and their housing spokesperson Darragh O'Brien indicated that he was open to reviewing the party's position on the matter.

In 2018 an opinion poll commissioned by the Irish Human Rights and Equality Commission confirmed the findings of the Constitutional Convention. The poll found that 82 percent of people generally and 89 percent of 18–24-year-olds believed that housing should be considered a human right. When asked if that right should be enshrined into the Constitution 63 percent generally and 78 percent of 18–24-year-olds believed it should.[15]

As should be clear from the discussion above, a legal right to housing is an important tool in ensuring people have access to appropriate, secure and affordable homes. It does not interfere in the right of democratically elected politicians to make decisions about how the right should be realised, nor does it interfere in the separation of powers between the legislature and judiciary.

Rather, just like political rights which are already in our Constitution, it would create a clear legal framework within which Governments must act to progressively realise people's right to a home.

The term 'progressively realise' is also important, as passing a constitutional amendment guaranteeing a right to housing does not mean that the following day all citizens are automatically entitled to a house provided by the State. Rather it means that Government, when framing policies and budgets, must consider how to ensure that those who currently do not have access to appropriate, secure and affordable housing can come to do so.

So just as Government must consult the Attorney General on all legislation to ensure it does not contravene existing rights provisions in the Constitution, including the right to private property, so too would they have to check future legislation against the right to housing.

Such a constitutional right would also help in promoting an important cultural shift away from thinking of housing as a commodity and towards an understanding of housing as, in the first and primary instance, a home, a social good rather than a financial asset.

Any serious attempt to fix our dysfunctional housing system must rest on providing a legal right to a home. And what better way to do that than to hold a constitutional referendum on the matter and let the people decide whether they want that protection or not.

Right to Housing Proposal

- Enact legislation to hold a referendum asking the people to enshrine the right to housing in the Constitution

---

Why Public Housing is the Answer

A legal right to a home will not in and of itself meet the housing needs of the growing number of households left behind by the private market. This requires direct State intervention in the provision of public housing.

Historically, public housing in an Irish context has meant housing provided by the State through Local Authorities or the not-for-profit sector acting on behalf of the State and with public funds. As detailed earlier this was, in the first instance, subsidised housing for working-class communities which subsequently became increasingly residualised, providing subsidised housing for the unemployed and those in precarious employment.

However, what really defines public housing is not, in the first instance, who it is for. Rather its unique feature is that it is non-market housing. It is the non-market nature of the accommodation that enables the State or its agents to provide housing at affordable levels to those unable to access market housing or for those in market housing but struggling with affordability issues.

On this basis public housing does not need to be, and indeed should not be, restricted just to the very poorest in our society. In many other countries public housing is provided to a much broader mix of households with a wider range of income levels and economic circumstances than has been the case here.

If we are serious about meeting social and affordable housing need, while at the same time ensuring our housing system has a significant non-market buffer to help maintain stability into the future, then we need a completely new conception of public housing from what has dominated to date.

Public housing should be for all those people whose housing needs cannot be met by the market. And here housing need means access to an appropriate, secure and affordable home.

This would mean a public housing system that meets social housing need, i.e. housing subsidised by the State for households who cannot meet the economic cost of their own homes and non-subsidised housing for those households who can meet the economic cost of the provision and maintenance of the property but for whom the additional cost involved in private housing – i.e. costs of land, developers' profit, additional costs of finance, etc. – make private housing unaffordable.

The definition of affordable in this context would be both the Central Bank's mortgage lending rule of 3.5 percent of gross household income for home purchasers and a 30 percent of net disposable income for renting households, possibly with a slightly lower percentage for lower-income households just above the threshold for differential rent. Those currently experiencing difficulties with these affordability criteria are, in the main, households with an annual gross income of between €40,000 and €75,000.

Such non-subsidised public housing could be affordable cost rental accommodation, as advocated by NESC in 2004 and the Nevin Economic Research Institute in 2017 and as currently provided in many continental European cities.[16] While NESC recommended that cost rental housing should be provided by not-for-profit or low-profit providers there is no reason why it could not be directly provided by Local Authorities.

Non-subsidised public housing could also be provided for purchase, though with a number of important caveats. Homeownership is not enshrined in our DNA, we do not have a cultural predisposition to this form of tenure. Rather, a century of housing policy has promoted homeownership as the only long-term, secure and affordable form of housing available to most people. The relegation of the private rental sector and post-1970s of the social rented sector has reaffirmed this reality.

As a consequence, many people today do prefer homeownership. Therefore, as affordable cost rental is rolled out on a scale necessary to meet demand there will be those who still want to purchase a home at an affordable rate.

So how can a public housing system accommodate this desire for private homeownership? Firstly, the land on which the affordable purchase home sits should never be sold, rather it should be leased to the homeowner indefinitely at no or low cost. This would remove a significant element from the purchase price of the property. Secondly, there should be a contractual requirement preventing the property from ever being sold into the private market. The owner can pass it on to their children and grandchildren but at whatever point the owners wish to sell, it must be sold back into the affordable housing scheme at the current discounted price adjusted for home improvement.

This model of affordable purchase housing has been developed by Ó Cualann Co-Housing Alliance in partnership with the local community in Poppintree, Ballymun since 2017.[17] It provides high-quality two- and three-bedroom homes for a purchase price between €170,000 and €225,000 at a time when the average market price in Dublin City was between €340,000 and €400,000.[18]

The difference in the price is as a result of a number of costs being excluded from the sales price including land, site servicing, Council development levies, developers' margin and high financing costs associated with private sector developments.

While Ó Cualann properties can be sold into the private market, through with a significant clawback if the sale takes place within a certain period of time, this was not their preferred option. However, as they are reliant on private bank finance for both the construction and mortgage finance it was not possible to prohibit sale in this way.

Nevertheless, Local Authorities utilising their own land and financing could provide affordable purchase housing on the basis outlined above, and thus facilitate those households who would prefer to purchase than rent. Essentially the home buyer would be purchasing the bricks and mortar of the house at its economic cost. As they would neither own the land on which the property sits nor be able to avail of house and land price increases due to public or private investments in the surrounding areas there would be no subsidy involved in the provision of the housing.

This broader conception of public housing, incorporating subsidised social rental, non-subsidised affordable cost rental and non-subsidised affordable purchase, would mean that a much broader mixture of households would be able to access good quality, secure and affordable accommodation outside the market. If delivered at a sufficient scale it would also provide eligible households with real alternatives to the private market thus promoting a genuinely tenure neutral system.

So who would live in these homes? They would be the temporarily unemployed and those permanently outside the labour market. They would be those in precarious, part-time or low-paid employment. They would also be those earning stable, modest and above average incomes, whether working class or lower middle class. They would be students, carers and pensioners. They would be people in a range of manual, service and clerical professions, of different ages, abilities and aspirations. Instead of social housing for the poor we would have public housing for a diverse range of people, all of whose housing needs are not currently met by the private market.

One of the values of this model of public housing is that not only do you strive to meet social and affordable housing need but you do it in a way that allows for the creation of genuinely mixed-income communities.

The discourse of mixed tenure, common to housing policies in many countries and first incorporated into Southern Irish housing policy in the 1991 *A Plan for Social Housing*, is deeply problematic. It has become a blind article of faith that large-scale public housing is inherently bad, inevitably producing ghettos, and therefore to be avoided. This is despite important evidence to the contrary from leading social housing policy experts, most notably in Tony Fahey's *Social Housing in Ireland* published in 1997 and more recently by Byrne, Norris and Carnegie in 2018.[19]

The arguments underpinning the dogma of mixed tenure serve to misrepresent the vast majority of Local Authority estates, which are good places to live, with vibrant communities and sustainable economic bases. It is deeply patronising to working-class communities. Fahey rightly points out that Council tenants 'would probably resent the implication that they required an infusion of middle-class households and middle-class values in order to bring their neighbourhoods up to satisfactory standards'.[20]

The findings of this landmark study on social housing rightly challenged the assumptions underlying *A Plan for Social Housing*, and indeed all subsequent Government housing policy documents, when it concluded that

There is no justification for assuming that large-scale housing provision by local authorities (or by other social housing providers such as voluntary housing agencies) is misguided or doomed to widespread failure or should be drastically scaled back or abandoned by present or future housing policy.[21]

Indeed, the study, which was based on extensive field research on seven social housing estates across the State, including hundreds of interviews with Council tenants, strongly recommended to Government that 'new social housing provision should be increased to the level required to meet present need'.[22]

The problem with the dogma of mixed tenure, as articulated in current housing policy discourse, is that it conflates high concentrations of poverty with mono-tenure. Of course, as other public housing systems clearly demonstrate, this doesn't have to be the case. As detailed earlier, the increasing concentration of low-income, economically vulnerable households in specific Council estates was the direct result of housing policy decisions taken by Government. In turn, as policy encouraged the flight of more economically secure households from inner city or suburban communities such as O'Devaney Gardens, St Michael's Estate, Ballymun or Fettercairn, these same communities were griped with the scourge of heroin. The State's subsequent failure to respond adequately to the realities of socio-economic deprivation and organised crime caused further decline.

The problem in these neighbourhoods – which were a minority of Council estates – was not the lack of mixed tenure, but the State's refusal to address high unemployment and high levels of crime through sustained investment, community empowerment and adequate policing.

However, the dogma of mixed tenure is not only based on a misunderstanding of the successes and failures of social housing during the 1970s and 1980s. It is also a convenient justification for the reductions in direct public expenditure that Governments made from 1987 onwards. Closing down the option of large-scale Local Authority developments on grounds of wanting to avoid the creation of ghettos is a convenient way of concealing the State's abdication of its responsibilities to directly provide appropriate, secure and affordable housing for those whose needs are not met by the market.

Crucially, by abandoning large-scale public house building, Government policy forced ever greater numbers of people into reliance on the private rental sector through State subsidies or on the Approved Housing Body sector which, until 2018, funded ever greater portions of its output from private finance and was thus off the Government's balance sheet.

While the authors of the NESC *Development Welfare State* report in 2005 and those officials in the Department of Housing influenced by this key document were no doubt convinced of the social policy arguments on their own merits, it is hard not to conclude that the real attraction of the mixed tenure discourse for politicians in Government was that it gave them policy cover to justify expenditure decisions which would have the opposite effect than that claimed, i.e. reducing the State's capacity to meet housing need rather than enhancing it.

The key issue here is not tenure mix but income mix and the public housing model outlined above would be a far more effective way of generating real mixed-income communities comprised of social rental, cost rental and affordable purchase homes.

Indeed, a growing number of housing policy analysts are arguing that the dogma of mixed tenure – which seeks to insert small numbers of low-income families into private housing estates whether through mechanisms such as Part V acquisitions or subsidised private rental tenancies – may actually heighten social isolation, deepen division and exacerbate economic inequalities.[23]

What is also clear is that without large-scale State provision, neither the Approved Housing Body sector nor the private rental sector can provide either the volume of housing or the security of tenure that is required to meet current and future demand.

So whatever the merits of tenure mixing in theory, as it has been applied here it acts as a significant constraint on social housing delivery, as evidenced by growing Council waiting lists and ever longer waiting times for social housing allocations.

This raises the next question: if we are to abandon the dogma of mixed tenure and embrace a public housing model that seeks to meet a broader range of income groups through both subsidised and non-subsidised housing, how many units of accommodation do we actually need and how long would it take to deliver them?

With regard to social housing, calculating existing need is relatively straight forward, as the Department of Housing provides regular figures for the Local Authority Housing waiting lists as well as the numbers of households on RAS and HAP tenancies (those on Rent Supplement claims are included in the Council list figures).

This means we currently have an approximate real social housing need level of 135,000 households comprising of 71,000 households on Council lists as per the 2018 *Summary of Housing Need* published by the Housing Agency in addition to the 45,000 HAP and 19,000 RAS tenancies in place during the same period.

We do not have an accurate figure for the number of new applicants who come on to the Council housing lists each year. However, the *Summary of Housing Need* does provide a point-in-time figure for the number of households on the list less than twelve months. In 2018 the number was 14,461, in 2017 it was 15,797 with a similar figure recorded for 2016.

This figure would not include households who successfully applied for social housing during the year and then moved into a HAP tenancy prior to the *Summary of Housing Need* count. However, it does give us a rough estimate of the flow of households into housing need which allows us to have some way of projecting future demand.

Set against this we also need to consider the number of casual vacancies that come available each year as people move out of existing Council stock which is then relet to households on the housing list. Unfortunately the Department of Housing do not publish data on this but anecdotally it is understood that up to 3,000 such properties become available for allocation each year.

On this basis if no new social housing supports were provided and no new households came on to the list, over the next decade the existing real housing need would fall by 30,000. This means we need at least 100,000 new units to meet existing need, with an annual average output of 10,000 units.

In addition to this we would need units to meet the new need, i.e. those coming onto the housing list. While it is impossible to know what this future need would be, the figures provided by the Housing Agency demonstrate that an annual output of 10,000 units will not meet existing and new need and therefore must be exceeded.

It is possible that the State may need as many as 70,000 social houses over the next five years and as many as 140,000 over the course of the decade.

Calculating the number of households who are in need of affordable rental or purchase housing is much more difficult. There are no figures available from the Department of Housing or Housing Agency because there is no scheme for which people can apply for either affordable rental or purchase.

The 2004 NESC *Housing in Ireland* report, referencing a 1999/2000 Household Budget Survey estimated that 20 percent of all renters were paying more than 35 percent of their total household expenditure on rent.[24] The same report concluded that while mortgage affordability at that point in time did not seem to be a significant issue, changes in interest rates or earnings would result in challenges for many mortgage holders.

More recently the Economic and Social Research Institute in partnership with the Department of Housing have undertaken a study of affordability pressures in both the private rental and owner-occupier markets. Working Paper no. 593 published in June 2018 provides some tentative conclusions based on a detailed analysis of data ranging from 2005 to 2015. Their conclusions are significant and worth quoting in some detail. Among their key findings were the following observations:

> Households in the private rented sector, those living in Dublin (and the surrounding commuter regions) and those on low incomes face the greatest challenges. Indeed, private renter and mortgaged households in the lowest 25% of the income distribution pay on average two fifths of their income on housing costs.

> We find that throughout the period under evaluation, low income households (bottom 25% of the income distribution) who are in the private rental sector have always faced high housing payments, which suggest that affordability challenges are a structural rather than cyclical issue.

Using international definitions [of affordability], in 2014-2015 16% of households had high housing costs, but this figure was double for private renters and 70% for private renters and mortgaged households in the lowest quarter of the income distribution. It was particularly acute for private renters in the Dublin region where between 30 and 40% of households faced high housing costs.[25]

On the basis of this initial study we have a structural problem in which 16 percent of all households, 32 percent of renters and 70 percent of lower-income earners are experiencing significant affordability issues with their accommodation.

Again, it is very difficult to extrapolate concrete numbers from these conclusions, particularly for the mortgage holder sector. However, as a rough indicator for the private rental sector, there were 310,780 private rental tenancies in September 2018.[26] If 32 percent of these have high housing costs that equates to 99,449. Of course some of this number are high earners who are choosing higher-cost housing and have a larger disposable income.

Nevertheless, even this crude exercise demonstrates that there are very significant numbers of existing renters who are facing affordability problems. Given that a larger proportion of private renters are in lower-income brackets and that 70 percent of these households are paying up to 40 percent of their net disposable income on rent, there is no doubt that numbers involved are significant.

Thus any attempt, albeit on the basis of very limited data, to determine the level of current and future need for affordable public housing must conclude that we are looking at tens of thousands of units over a decade-long period, possibly as many as 45,000 over the next five years and ultimately 90,000 over the course of a decade.

Ultimately a comprehensive assessment of current and future housing need should be undertaken by the Department of Housing, with the assistance of the Housing Agency and the Central Statistics Office, to determine evidence-based figures that are reliable. However, it is not an unreasonable proposition that we will probably need something in the order of an additional 230,000 public housing units over the next ten years, with a greater weighting in favour of subsidised social housing.

Given that the Government's *National Development Plan* (NDP) estimates that an annual output of between 25,000 and 30,000 housing units are required, across all sectors, to meet existing and future housing need, this would mean public housing designed to meet social and affordable housing need would need to constitute approximately 50 percent of total output.

Equally if the NDP proposes the delivery of 112,000 public houses over the decade from 2018, then any plan that is to truly meet social and affordable housing need would need a target of at least double that figure.

This raises the question, how much would such a plan cost and where would the funding come from. In the first instance capital investment in the delivery of public housing to meet social and affordable need, owned and managed by Local Authorities and Approved Housing Bodies, would have to double from its current level of €1.1 billion in 2019 to at least €2.3 billion.

This would need to increase incrementally year on year as output increases to meet the agreed targets over the decade. The bulk of the funding would come from exchequer capital allocations, particularly in the initial years.

However, as the State's debt to GDP position improves this will enable greater public housing output to be funded through borrowings from the Housing Finance Agency, the European Investment Bank and the Credit Union Movement. Currently 70 percent of Approved Housing Body expenditure comes from the Housing Finance Agency or private bank lending.

The recent decision of the Department of Housing to allow Dublin City Council to fund the cost rental component of the proposed St Michael's Estate development with EIB funding demonstrates that for such projects loan finance for affordable rental mixed with exchequer capital finance for the social rental element may be most cost effective. However, this will require a restructuring of the loan at the end of the EIB's twenty-five/thirty-year period with the City Council taking on liability for a further period of time. Extending the provision of Capital Advance Loan Facility funds to Approved Housing Bodies for the purposes of providing affordable cost rental would also assist in this regard ensuring that a forty- to fifty-year combined loan maturity will allow entry rents that are genuinely affordable.

Government also needs to urgently review the way in which Local Authorities are funded through current expenditure to carry out their ongoing management and maintenance functions. Norris and Hayden in their important 2018 study *The Future of Council Housing* highlight the inefficiencies and perverse incentives in the current funding regime.[27] As differential rents do not cover the full cost of response and cyclical maintenance, there is a tendency for properties to be poorly maintained over the medium to long term, ultimately requiring expensive refurbishment or regeneration programmes.

While the authors of the report suggest replacing the differential rent system with a form of HAP payments for Council tenants, a better mechanism would be to fund the ongoing maintenance of Local Authority properties in the same way as Government funds Approved Housing Bodies, i.e. with a monthly availability agreement payment that covers the shortfall between the differential rent level and the full economic cost of the management and maintenance of the units, including provision of a sinking fund for cyclical upgrades.

While this would increase current expenditure allocations to Local Authorities, it would be cheaper than ongoing subsidised private rental tenancies such as HAP and RAS and would greatly reduce the long-term capital costs of stock maintenance. It could be phased in over a number of years so as to avoid placing too great an immediate burden on the exchequer. Importantly, at a certain point in time the loan element of the cost rental accommodation will be paid down in full making that accommodation a source of revenue which should be reinvested into the overall maintenance of the public housing stock.

Meeting such an expanded public housing delivery programme would require an acceleration of the planning, development and construction process, particularly in the initial years. This will require the Department of Finance and the Department of Housing making significant changes to the approval and procurement rules governing housing delivery.

The first would mean a shortening of the pre- and post-planning approval and capital appraisal processes which currently add a significant length of time to the pre-construction development timeline. This would mean Central Government trusting Local Authorities to do the job they are tasked to do and reducing the level of duplication in project design, plan approval and cost appraisal. This process, from start to finish, including Part 8 planning, must be shortened to six months.

Alongside this there needs to be greater use of framework agreements for the procurement of design and build contractors. Forcing Local Authorities to go to tender for every design or build contract is incredibly time-consuming. Rather Councils, either on their own in the case of larger Local Authorities or in regional clusters for the smaller ones, should procure lists of approved contractors on a three- or five-years basis, possibly disaggregated for developments of different sizes. This would mean a single, big bang, tendering process once every three to five years, after which contractors are selected from the shelf.

There is also a clear rationale for exploring the possibility of a return to direct build by Local Authorities or the creation of a statewide or regional public building companies. While the establishment of direct build would take time, there is no reason why it could not be piloted in a single, possibly mid-sized Local Authority such as Cork City, in order to determine its cost effectiveness.

In terms of who is best placed to deliver such an ambitious programme of public housing delivery there is some difference of opinion. Some think tanks such as the Nevin Economic Research Institute and political parties such as Labour and Social Democrats have called for a new State or semi-State Agency tasked with delivering a more ambitious programme of social and/or cost rental accommodation, partly to take advantage of EU off-balance sheet rules. Others, including the sector themselves, would like to see the Approved Housing Bodies play a greater role.

However, creating a new State Agency would take time and may be less responsive to the dynamics of local need than a more devolved approach. There is also a strong argument for ensuring that housing delivery is subject to democratic approval and oversight at a local level, which is best achieved by well-functioning Local Authorities.

Also, caution should be taken when considering off-balance sheet mechanisms of delivery as EU requirements mean such mechanisms must operate as market actors with obvious risks for delivering genuine affordability. Equally the capacity of the Approved Housing Body sector remains low and though that is expected to improve in the coming years its role will continue to be supplementary to that of the State.

Given the successful role of Local Authorities in delivering significant quantities of good quality social housing in the past there is no reason this could not be revived. The issue is whether Central Government is willing to provide the necessary resources, including staff as well as capital and current funding, to allow this to happen. The supporting role of the Housing Agency and the greater development of shared services on a regional level between Councils would also be required.

Approved Housing Bodies would continue to have an important role, delivering approximately 2,000 units a year in the short term and ultimately increasing this to 4,000 homes a year. However, caution should be expressed with respect to the price to be paid to get the sectors borrowings and spending off-balance sheet. The Eurostat reclassification has removed one of the primary benefits for Government to utilise the not-for-profit sector for general needs public housing provision. It is clearly preferable for Approved Housing Bodies not to be on balance sheet, but only if they are able to maintain their non-market nature and not-for-profit ethos.

Eurostat expressed concern at the fact that the Approved Housing Bodies' principal aim gave them a 'non-market nature', that the rents were not economically significant and did not respond to market 'signals' and that they 'have little influence' on the sector's investment decisions.[28] Reversing or weakening these fundamental features of the sector would put them on a pathway to becoming commercial rather than not-for-profit providers. It would be preferable for them to remain on balance sheet than take such a risk.

There is also a need to address the issue of the long-term future of Approved Housing Body stock. Under current arrangements once the initial CAS/CLSS/CALF loan is paid down, the stock and its use is exclusively a matter for the social landlord. Strictly speaking the board of an AHB could decide to dispose of the asset or shift it into commercial or semi-commercial use. Given that the unit was paid for with public funds this is not ideal and should be addressed to protect the public interest.

It is important to stress that no Approved Housing Body is currently proposing such disposals or changes of use when the first generation of CAS/CLSS loans mature in the coming years. But that does not mean that future Boards of Directors or CEOs could not propose such action.

The mainstream private sector should also continue to provide social and affordable housing through the provision of discounted units under Part V of the Planning and Development Act. However, the percentage must be increased from the reduced level of 10 percent of a development as introduced by Fine Gael and Labour in 2014 to at least 20 percent and possibly 25 percent in all standard developments and 30 percent in Strategic Development Zones. The Dáil passed a Sinn Féin Private Members Bill to achieve this very objective in November 2018 following an agreement with Fianna Fáil to amend the Bill in Committee stage.[29]

Nevertheless, strict limits on the extent of private sector involvement in the delivery of public housing must be imposed. As stated above it is the non-market nature of public housing that enables it to be provided at an affordable rate to those unable to access market housing. While public housing is not completely insulated from all market effects – use of private builders or accessing market finance albeit at low interest rates via the HFA and EIB are cases in point – caution must be taken to ensure that market dynamics do not undermine the ability of public housing to meet its core objective.

Public Private Partnerships, Joint Ventures, public land sales, stock transfers, private rental subsidies and long-term leasing arrangements all introduce ever greater levels of profit maximisation, increasing costs and undermining the long-term benefits of public housing to both tenants and the taxpayer. Current policy promotion of such mechanisms should be reversed to withdraw as quickly as is practicably possible from all such financial arrangements.

This would mean in the first instance no future adoption of such funding mechanisms for new projects and the phased withdrawal from those already in existence either during or at the conclusion of the current lease or partnership period. Clearly existing contractual commitments would have to be honoured where a cost-effective withdrawal is not possible.

It would also mean that rental subsidies would no longer be seen as a long-term social housing solution. Instead they would revert to being a temporary or transitional support for those on public housing waiting lists for social and affordable housing, for young people yet to decide on their preferred long-term housing option, or for those who, due to temporary illness or unemployment, need assistance with the payment of rent.

A simplified system with a single Housing Benefit paid by the Local Authorities would be preferable to the existing Rent Supplement, RAS, HAP and private sector SHCEP schemes, for tenants, landlords and public administration.

The recently created Land Development Agency would also require significant amendment. While as outlined earlier its strategic land management functions are welcome and long overdue, its application of the Joint Venture funding model and restriction of the public housing element to just 40 percent (10 percent social and 30 percent affordable) is not compatible with a real public housing programme.

A better configuration for the Agency would be to allow it to keep its land acquisition and management functions and, where residential development is to take place, this should be done in partnership with Local Authorities and Approved Housing Bodies funded through standard public housing financing mechanisms.

This, of course, would mean its developments would be on balance sheet. However, if it is a choice between meeting social and affordable housing need in the medium to long term or reducing the State's debt and deficit levels in the short term, proper housing and social policy considerations dictate that the former should take precedence over the latter.

Thus what we are talking about is both large and small scale public housing developments on public land, funded through revenue allocations and low interest long-term HFA, EIB and Credit Union finance, with mixed-income housing to meet subsidised social rental, non-subsidised affordable cost rental and where appropriate non-subsidised but permanently affordable purchase housing, delivered by Local Authorities and Approved Housing Bodies, on a scale commensurate with current and emerging social and affordable housing need.

Such a model of public housing would require a fundamental review of some of the key features of our current social housing schemes. What should be the eligibility criteria to access such housing, particularly in terms of income thresholds? What of the allocations schemes, already in bad need of reform and a greater level of flexibility to allow prospective tenants to move from one Local Authority to another without penalty? At what income point should subsidised social rental end and non-subsidised cost rental start? Would social rental tenants shift to cost rental rents if their incomes rose above the social housing threshold during the lifetime of their tenancy? Would there be a single-cost rent or bands linking the rent to income to guarantee affordability with an element of cross-subsidisation between cost rental tenants to ensure that the full cost of provision and maintenance is recovered? Would the differential and cost rental systems merge over time into a more complex tiered form of income linked rent?

And what of tenant purchase? If affordable purchase homes should not be sold into the private market then surely the same rule should apply to purchase of social rental properties? If the State was providing a stream of affordable purchase homes would there be a rationale for tenant purchase at all?

Answering all of these questions is beyond the scope of this book, however they are issues of significant importance which need to be considered.

One of the positive unintended consequences of the public housing policy outlined above is that it would also significantly reduce pressure on the private rental sector increasing supply and reducing costs for renters and indeed for first-time buyers. The 100,000 private rental properties currently occupied by HAP, Rent Supplement and RAS tenants would be gradually freed up, making space for private renters and home buyers.

There would also be a need to ensure a greater provision of student-specific accommodation, in both the public and private sectors, than that envisioned in the current Government student accommodation strategy in order to address the 20,000 bed-space shortfall in that plan.

The 2004 NESC *Housing in Ireland* report, discussing the influential work of housing policy specialist Jim Kemeny, spoke of the distinction in the academic literature between unitary and dualist rental markets. Unitary systems, such as those in Germany and Austria, were broadly tenure neutral and provided a significant portion of non-market rental properties. In contrast, predominantly Anglo-Saxon economies such as Ireland, Britain and Australia tend to privilege owner-occupation and have a very clear demarcation between a small public housing system for the poor and a much larger private rental and purchase sector for the majority.

While the report stopped short of advocating a shift from the dualist model to the unitary model, one gets the impression when reading the document that this is not because the authors would not like to see such a shift, but rather that they did not think it was politically possible given the balance of forces in the Oireachtas at that time.

However, the unitary model is not without its problems. The concept of social-market operators is a tricky one, opening the non-market sector to market dynamics which could undermine its ability to meet social and affordable housing need, particularly for those with lowest incomes or least able to access secure and affordable accommodation.

The public housing programme outlined here, rather than abandoning the dualist model, seeks to expand the non-market component to that of an equal player, thus balancing the system overall while meeting social and affordable housing need. It adopts the best elements of both the unitary and dualist systems and applies them to the specific historic context of the Southern Irish housing system as it exists today.

Whatever one calls it, the arguments in favour of a fundamental shift in the design of our housing system are

---

Public Housing Proposal

- Commission the National Economic and Social Council to undertake a second *Housing in Ireland* study
- Change the legal definition of public housing to include social, affordable rental and affordable purchase housing
- Outline a 10-year programme for delivery of up to 145,000 social and 90,000 affordable homes
- Immediately double capital investment with incremental annual increases to fund the programme
- Reform the current funding of public housing to promote better maintenance of stock
- Reform all rental subsidies for social housing tenants into a single Housing Benefit
- Amend Capital Advance Loan Facility loans to support provision of affordable housing

compelling. Given the level of detailed quantitative work that would be required to provide an adequate evidence base for such a shift, it would be necessary to commission the National Economic and Social Council to undertake a new *Housing in Ireland* study with terms of reference explicitly seeking guidance on how to transform our dysfunctional housing system into one which provides appropriate, secure and affordable housing for all those left behind by the failures of past and current policy.

Reforming the Private Rental Sector

A second NESC *Housing in Ireland* report could also examine in detail the significant changes that have occurred within the private rental sector since the late 1990s. A combination of increased social housing subsidised tenancies and house price inflation forcing modest and above average working households to rent for longer periods of time has seen the sector increase in size from 9 percent of total housing stock in 1991 to 18 percent in 2016.

As of September 2018 there are 310,780 private rental tenancies registered with the Residential Tenancies Board in which 675,622 people live.[30] While one in five people now live in the private rental sector, in Dublin almost a third of all households rent.

One of the unusual features of the Southern Irish rental market is the large volume of semi-professional or accidental landlords. Almost 80 percent of the 172,820 landlords operating in the State own just one property. Many of these are people who availed of Celtic Tiger lending to buy a second home primarily as a passive investment. Others took advantage of generous Section 23 tax reliefs when purchasing buy-to-let mortgages. However, a lack of appreciation that being a landlord is an active investment requiring a significant allocation of time rather than passive investment, had meant that many landlords did not fully understand the scale of the undertaking they were engaging in.

In addition to the large number of semi-professional landlords there are those for whom renting emerged from necessity as negative equity prevented them from selling their initial family home when up-sizing. Caught in this bind they rented out their own home while either paying a second mortgage secured with the collateral of the first house or becoming renters themselves moving into larger private rental accommodation.

The regulatory context in which landlords and tenants operate is complex. The 2004 Residential Tenancies Act, which deals with issues of tenure, rent setting and dispute resolution, has been subject to three separate sets of amendments in 2009, 2015 and 2016 as well as a range of consequent regulations introduced by way of statutory instrument. Two further significant sets of amendments are due in 2019.

While responsibility for mediating and adjudicating on the issues contained in this body of legislation rests with the Residential Tenancies Board, issues of minimum standards and compliance inspections are the responsibility of Local Authorities.

The complex and frequently changing legal and institutional framework governing the rental sector can be confusing for both tenants and many semi-professional and accidental landlords. The amateur nature of many landlords and the vulnerable nature of many low-income tenants has meant that, legislation and regulations notwithstanding, many landlords and tenants do not understand what their rights and obligations are or how to go about ensuring that they are protected.

While significant work is carried out both by the Residential Tenancies Board itself, and on behalf of tenants by NGOs such as Threshold and grass roots organisations such as the Dublin Tenants Association, the environment can be confusing and at times contradictory.

For tenants the key issues today, particularly in the large urban centres, are the excessive and still rising rents, alongside issues of tenure length and security. However, there are also very significant issues of quality and poor standards especially at the lower end of the market. Local Authority inspection rates are in the main low and they record a very high level of non-compliance. While some compliance issues are minor, others such as those exposed in the 2017 *RTÉ Investigates* 'Nightmare to Let' documentary are at the very extreme end.

For many accidental and semi-professional landlords with mortgage arrears, the recent revival in house prices has incentivised an exit from the market either by choice or under pressure from their lenders. According to the RTB a total of 9,000 rental properties left the market from January 2017 to September 2018, the first sustained reduction in recent decades.

There are also very significant variances in the tax treatment of landlords with accidental and semi-professional landlords often paying high effective rates of tax while larger institutional investors pay zero tax on their rent role or capital gains; investors also only have to pay a 20 percent dividend tax if resident in the State.

Rebuilding Ireland committed Government 'to developing a real and meaningful strategy for the rental sector to enable it to reach its full potential'.[31] The strategy was to provide 'a vision for what role we want and expect the sector to play over the short, medium and long term'.

The twenty-six page plan was published six months later in December 2016. The then Minister for Housing Simon Coveney described the private rental sector as 'broken' and 'unattractive'.[32] The strategy identified affordability as the most immediate challenge that would ultimately be addressed by increasing supply. However, interim measures to constrain rental inflation would also be required.

The promise of the plan was threefold. To create 'stability, quality and choice' for tenants while ensuring a 'stable investment climate' for landlords and to 'simplify' regulations for the benefits of both parties.[33]

However, the detail of the plan was underwhelming, to say the least. Its four sections – security, supply, standards and service – outlined a small number of concrete actions and a larger number of general or aspirational commitments. The most concrete of measures was the introduction of Rent Pressure Zones, which, as detailed earlier, placed a 4 percent cap on annual rent increases in most urban and commuter belt areas in the State, which by mid-2017 covered over half of all rental tenancies.

However, other measures dealing with supply, such as commitment to bring vacant units back into use, to roll out a build-to-rent model or the long-promised cost rental pilot, have so far not been delivered.

Likewise promises to provide a new standards regime or a deposit protection system have not been implemented, while commitments to increase Local Authority inspection rates have been stretched out to 2021 and beyond. The commitment to increase mortgage interest relief for landlords has been enacted but other measures, such as fast-tracking evictions for tenants in significant arrears, have not.

As with the original recommendations of the Commission on the Private Rental Sector in 1999 both tenants and landlords remain unhappy with the status quo, which is unlikely to change significantly on the basis of the content of the Government's strategy.

The core problem of the strategy is that it lacks any long-term vision or a series of specific short-, medium- and long-term reforms that would be required to transform the private rental sector from its current dysfunctional state into a sector where people would willingly choose to live for long periods of time.

In outlining what an alternative strategy should look like it is important to make clear that our housing system needs a private rented sector both to meet the short-term housing needs of specific types of households and to provide long-term housing to those with adequate incomes who are either not able or who do not want to purchase.

The key to a functioning private rental sector is that it must provide good quality, secure and affordable accommodation to tenants while allowing landlords and investors to make a reasonable rate of return for the service they provide. Such a sector must be clearly regulated, with effective policing and enforcement mechanisms and due process available to both tenants and landlords.

Given that a third of current private rental lets are to subsidised social housing tenants and up to 30 percent of non-subsidised private rental tenants have affordability issues, the implementation of a decade-long public housing programme as outlined above should see a significant reduction of the size of the private rental sector.

While some prospective first-time buyers may find a secure long-term rental market attractive, thus shifting the balance between owner-occupation and private rental, it is estimated that a functioning housing system would need at least 10 percent of its total stock to be for private rent.

At the core of a functioning rental market must be security of tenure. This would require the introduction of tenancies of indefinite duration as the standard and the removal of Section 34 grounds for issuing Notices to Quit such as occupation by landlord or a family member or sale of property. While tenancy termination for non-payment of rent or another breach of contract would remain on the statute, the fundamental principal that a tenant remains in situ for as long as they require subject to meeting the terms of their tenancy agreement is the only way to ensure long-term stability.

While shorter license agreements for students, temporary workers or specific accommodation arrangements would be available, long-term and even lifetime tenure is only possible if tenancies of indefinite duration are detailed in and protected by law.

Alongside security of tenure must sit rent certainty. While the current spiralling cost of rents requires a number of emergency measures, a functioning rental market should link rents to some form of index such as the Consumer Price Index and limit rent reviews to periodic intervals. Rent certainty is good for both landlords and tenants in that it gives clarity and security into the future.

In the short term, however, there is a need for an immediate three-year rent freeze to prevent rents from increasing. This would replace the Rent Pressure Zones, would apply statewide and would be subject to an automatic sunset clause replacing the freeze with index-linked rent certainty at the end of its term. The freeze would apply to all existing and new tenancies to the market, the latter set at rent levels according to the Standardised RTB index in their respective county or Local Electoral Area from the date the freeze comes into operation. There would be no exemptions.

However, while a rent freeze will stop future rent increases it will not help those tenants whose current rent levels are already too high. To achieve a reduction in existing rents Government has three available policy options. An emergency rent reduction imposed by law on all existing rental agreements; an income supplement paid to all qualifying tenants; or a refundable tax relief for renters.

An emergency rent reduction imposed by legislation could take a form similar to the Financial Emergency Measures in the Public Interest legislation used to cut public sector pay from 2009. The basic proposition would be to peg rents at a point in time when they were lower. However, such a move would likely result is a significant volume of legal challenges from landlords. It is hard to see how it could be defended legally insofar as it would be general in application (i.e. to all landlords and not just those with excessive rents) and no compensation would be provided for loss of earnings (as would otherwise be the case when for example the State uses Compulsory Purchase Order powers).

While the Constitution allows for restrictions to private property rights when such limitations are to protect the common good and in accordance with principles of social justice, any such restrictions need to be proportionate and fair. One could seek to amend the Constitution to allow the State to regulate private contracts in this way, though given the need for immediate relief for renters and the widescale implications for large sectors of the economy of such a change, such a proposal would take too long and would be difficult to win.

Alternatively, the Department of Housing could provide an income supplement to households struggling with their rents, similar to Family Income Supplement, currently paid by the Department of Social Protection to low-income working families. Setting income thresholds and rent levels for eligible tenants would be relatively straightforward. However, if such a payment was to be means tested its application could be bureaucratic and prohibitively expensive.

A third option would be to provide renters with a refundable tax relief equivalent to 8.3 percent of rent paid in the previous year capped at the statewide average rent as per the RTBs rent index. This would be much easier to administer and would avoid the potential legal challenges from landlords. It could reduce the annual cost of rents to the average household by up to €1,500 a year.

If the three-year rent freeze were combined with the three-year refundable tax relief alongside an ambitious programme of public house building – increasing supply of cost rental and availability of standard private rental due to a shift of social housing tenants from rental subsidies to standard social housing – private rental supply and in turn rents should start to return to pre-peak levels by the time the freeze and relief expire.

While a legal challenge to the rent freeze is equally likely, given the high level of rents, it would be a much stronger case to fight in the courts, particularly given its temporary nature.

Providing long-term security of tenure and rent certainty must also be accompanied by a third fundamental reform, ensuring proper standards. While some legislative work is required to update definitions of serious overcrowding, the key improvements must be in the areas of policing and enforcement.

The 2017 National Oversight and Audit Commission's *Local Authority Performance Indicator Report* provides a detailed breakdown of private sector rental property inspections by Council area, including the total number of rental tenancies, the number of inspections and the level of compliance.[34]

What it shows is a low rate of inspections and a high rate of non-compliance. The compliance levels are skewed by virtue of the fact that some Local Authorities prioritise inspections of older properties while others only inspect on foot of a complaint. However, the low inspection rate is harder to explain. Though significant staff reductions since 2008 may be a factor, pre-recession inspection rates were also low.

In response to the heightened public profile of the issue of standards the Government has committed to resourcing Local Authorities to achieve a 25 percent inspection rate of all rental properties by 2021. Given that the total cost of this measure is just €10 million it is hard to understand why this could not have been achieved in a shorter time scale.

A more robust system would be to introduce an NCT-style certification system for all private rental properties in which a certificate of compliance with building, fire safety and energy requirements is available to tenants in advance of letting and a copy of which is legally required for registration of a tenancy with the RTB. The Local Authorities would provide the certification.

This could be phased in over four years for existing tenancies, assuming a 25 percent inspection rate starting from the current year, while making it mandatory for all new lets. The cost of the inspection would be borne by the landlord at an estimated price of €100 and would be renewed every fifth year.

By 2021 all rental properties would be inspected and provided with a standards compliance certificate at a low cost to the landlord and at zero cost to the taxpayer. This would not only give tenants the reassurance they need that the property meets regulations, but would also prevent unscrupulous landlords from undercutting reputable service providers by cutting costs. Non-compliance with the NCT, like non-compliance with the RTB registration, would be subject to a significant fine on foot of the presentation of an inspection report to the RTB.

These three changes would transform the private rental sector in a meaningful way ensuring that tenants have security of tenure, rent certainty and good quality accommodation.

In exchange for these improvements in tenants' rights a number of important reforms on the landlord side are also needed. In the first instance we need to accept that the large cohort of accidental and non-professional landlords are part of the reason for the dysfunctional nature of the system.

While deliberately unscrupulous landlords are undoubtedly a problem, the prevalence of amateur landlords, unsure of their legal responsibilities, unable to invest the time required to provide a proper service, and constrained by significant liabilities on their rental and at times private home, is a much greater difficulty.

We have to accept that over a period of time these landlords either must professionalise or exit the market. Given that this is already happening, though in an unplanned and disorganised fashion, Government policy must make this transition an objective, and support those landlords who want to remain.

This will require a mandatory professional training and accreditation requirement for landlords to be introduced. It is remarkable that other service providers such as taxi drivers and pub or nightclub security workers require qualifications and certification to be able to trade. Such a system is needed for landlords. For those unwilling to or unable to undertake such a role, an enhanced and properly regulated landlord function for estate agents, who would enter into long term-lease agreements with property owners, could also be provided.

Contrary to the argument of some, a fully professionalised landlord sector does not have to exclude single property owners, as demonstrated in the case of Germany. However, the crucial shift is for landlords to understand not only the ongoing time commitment required for adequate service provision but that their investment is active and based on ongoing returns rather than a once-off capital gain when the property is sold. Ultimately rental properties must become rental properties in perpetuity with exit from the market strictly regulated and controlled.

The Residential Tenancies Board is already involved in voluntary training. Nevertheless, until Government makes this mandatory, with an appropriate medium-term lead time, it will remain peripheral to the sector.

There is also a need for a reform of the tax treatment of landlords. Governments past and present have made significant use of tax breaks to incentivise investment into the private rental sector. From Section 23 Reliefs and Mortgage Interest Relief for Landlords to the excessively generous tax treatment of REIT's and ICAV's, a substantial amount of tax has been forgone to create a rental system that the previous Housing Minister described as 'broken'. Taxpayers would be right to ask if they have received value for money from this lost revenue.

However, there are also significant differences in the tax treatment of different classes of landlords, with many accidental and semi-professional landlords paying more than 50 percent of their rental income on tax while well-constructed 'tax efficient' investment funds legally avoid paying any tax.

A more sensible arrangement would be to create a single tax regime for all landlords. Such a regime should treat their rental income as turnover rather than taxable revenue and establish a single system of offsets for all landlords relating to staff costs, maintenance, repair and upgrade. A standard state of landlord-specific tax should then be levied on profits. Careful consideration should be given to the rate at which this tax should be set. Mortgage interest relief for landlords should be ended on the introduction of this new regime.

Such a system would allow landlords who provide a good quality of service to their tenants to make a fair return on their time and investment. Some landlords, due to outstanding liabilities, may not be able to operate in such a reformed system, others may not be willing. In both cases their investments should rest elsewhere.

There is no reason why all of the reforms detailed above could not be implemented in a single piece of legislation. This could also include a number of smaller reforms such as increasing the ability of the Residential Tenancies Board to enforce its determinations more quickly, particularly in the case of evictions for wilful non-payment of rent by tenants or breach of contract by landlords and a deposit protection scheme.

Private Rental Sector Proposal

- Introduce an omnibus Residential Tenancies (Amendment) Bill to provide tenancies of indefinite duration and rent certainty with tougher sanctions for wilful breach of contract and an NCT certification for standards
- Include emergency provisions in the Bill to provide for a rent freeze and refundable tax credit with a three-year sunset clause
- Amend the tax treatment of landlords to create a single tax regime with a set rate of tax on profits while ceasing Mortgage Interest Relief for landlords
- Fund Local Authorities to ensure a mandatory 25 percent inspection rate for all rental properties annually

---

Government also needs to consider very carefully what kind of investment it wants to see in the rental sector into the future. All reliefs targeting short-term investment funds (vulture funds) must cease. A stable rental market needs investors who are there for the long term, financing, building and managing properties for the sole purpose of generating a reasonable 2 to 3 percent annual return on their investment, guaranteed for decades. Government policy should be focused on pension funds, Credit Unions and other low-risk, long-term investors rather than the high-risk, short-term business model of many REITs and ICAVs.

Regulating the Private Purchase Sector

The 2008 financial crash was at its heart a crash in property prices. Not only did values collapse but so too did the construction industry. In 2006, the high point of Celtic Tiger output, 93,419 new homes were constructed. In 2012 just 4,907 completions took place. The numbers employed in the building and associated trades fell from 270,000 in 2007 to just 100,000 in 2012. Since then the number of completions has slowly edged upwards with 5,518 in 2014, 7,212 in 2015, 9,907 in 2016 and 14,435 in 2017.[35] Figures for the third quarter of 2018 show a further rise to 15,582.

Construction 2020, published by Government in 2014, listed 75 actions to get the sector back building again. It also estimated that the State would need at least 25,000 new homes a year for the foreseeable future to meet an estimated 20,000 new household formations annually alongside existing unmet demand. The target was repeated and extended slightly in the 2017 *National Development Plan* to between 25,000 and 30,000 new completions.

The most recent completion data from the Central Statistics Office (CSO) includes both new build homes and those brought back into use from vacant stock and Celtic Tiger era ghost estates (known as Unfinished Housing Developments, UFHDs). The data also separates out one-off housing from scheme (or housing estate) new builds.

In 2017 for example, from the total output of 18,000 dwellings, the number of new builds was 14,500, the number of returned vacant stock was 2,500 and the UFHDs were 1,000. Of the 14,500, 29 percent were one-off houses with the remainder mixed between 55 percent scheme houses and 16 percent apartments.

The CSO data includes both private and social housing completions with the latter accounting for approximately 28 percent including 2,245 new builds (including Part Vs) and 1,757 voids (though the latter figure is strongly disputed as it includes relet casual vacancies rather than long-term voids returned to stock).

Rebuilding Ireland's social housing new build targets (including Part Vs and voids) are set to increase annually from 3,200 in 2017 to 8,907 in 2021, meaning that if the overall *National Development Plan* house completion target is to be met the private sector output must reach between 16,093 and 21,093 completions.

While all housing completions are important because they provide much-needed homes for people, it is important to get a sense of where the construction industry is at and how likely it is to meet the NDP target. A good gauge of this is to strip out UFHDs and private sector vacants returned to stock and examine just the new builds. The rationale for this is that the number of remaining UFHD units are very low and returning private sector vacants even less. Thus if growth is to come, it must come from new construction.

In 2017 the new build dwelling figure was 14,500. Thus to meet the NDP targets private sector output must increase by as much as 45 percent in just three years. Some commentators such as Dublin Institute of Technology lecturer Lorcan Sirr and former chair of the Housing Agency Conor Skehan argue that a greater focus should be put on reducing the levels of obsolescence through better management of the existing housing stock, thus reducing the need for new build dwellings.[36] However whether through construction or refurbishment, on the basis of current trends meeting the NDP target, particularly at the upper end of 30,000, will be a real challenge.

In response Government has introduced a number of schemes to stimulate development and purchase. As discussed earlier the Help to Buy tax relief for first-time buyers is designed in part to boost supply. Likewise, the Local

Infrastructure Housing Activation Fund provides funds to private developers to help them unlock developments.

However, it is not clear whether either of these significant areas of Government expenditure are unlocking developments that would not have happened without financial assistance. There is no requirement to demonstrate this for accessing the tax relief while some of the largest LIHAF allocations (€15 million in Adamstown Co. Dublin and €20 million in Cherrywood Dún Laoghaire) have been to large-scale developers such as Hines and Castlethorn whose need for such support is highly questionable.

As of October 2018 the Help to Buy Scheme has cost the taxpayer €137 million in forgone revenue. The LIHAF allocation was initially €226 million (including a €56 million contribution from Local Authorities) with €75 million allocated from Central Government in 2018 and €205 million in 2019 following a €50 million increase. Both figures are set to rise in the years ahead.

In addition to the question of whether such investments are actually increasing the supply of new houses (rather than just reducing the developers' costs) there are also, as discussed above, significant question marks over whether any affordability dividend will be forthcoming.

One Department of Housing official confirmed to the author in an off-the-record conversation that little of the first round of LIHAF funding met either the eligibility or affordability criteria as the Department focused on getting the fund up and running. The official went on to say that the second round would be more focused on meeting the schemes stated intentions.

However, the real problem in private sector delivery lies in the interaction between viability and affordability, meaning that output at the higher end of the market is profitable but demand is lower. Making private housing affordable for modest and above average income households is both the greatest challenge and the biggest impediment to the private sector meeting their NDP targets.

Four important reports have been published in recent years exposing the depth of this challenge. In 2016 the Society of Chartered Surveyors of Ireland published a study on the all-in-development costs of house construction in Dublin. The report was based on eight live schemes and made for interesting reading. For a standard semi-detached house with a market value of €330,000 (at 2016 prices) the actual construction cost was just €122,000. If site servicing and development is included the total cost of the build was €150,000, or less than half the sales price.

The remainder of the development costs for the projects surveyed are broken down as follows: Land €57,900, VAT €37,000, developer's profit €38,000, cost of finance €20,000, Local Authority development levies €11,700, sales and marketing €8,200 and professional fees €5,500.

A second report from the institute published the following year examined the all-in-development costs for apartments in Dublin. The findings revealed an even more difficult picture.

In both reports a range of interventions were proposed to help reduce the cost of delivering houses and apartments, including: VAT and development levy reductions; reducing size, car parking and dual aspect requirements for apartments; providing lower-cost finance; and measures to reduce land costs.

However, on the basis of the figures provided in both reports, even if all of the proposed discounts were introduced by Government the homes, and in particular the apartments, would remain out of reach for most working households.

The 2017 report suggested that a two-bed apartment in a low-rise Dublin development with an all-in-development cost of between €330,000 and €387,000 could be offered at between €269,000 to €317,000 if all the proposed discounts were applied. A two-bed apartment in a medium-rise development in Dublin then priced at between €422,000 to €533,000 could be offered at between €321,000 to €412,000 if all the proposed discounts were offered.

While Government argues that the threshold for affordability is properties below €320,000 a more accurate figure, based on Central Bank macro-prudential lending rules for households on gross annual incomes of between €45,000 and €75,000, would be a range between €173,000 and €288,000. Thus the recommendations by the Chartered Surveyors would generate a small level of affordability at the top of the income range at best.

The overall picture from the two institute reports was confirmed by two Government reports published in 2018. The Housing Agency undertook a comparative study of construction costs which confirmed that the actual build costs here are broadly in line with comparable EU member States while a Department of Housing all-in-development cost survey simply restated the conclusions of the earlier surveys.

What all four reports show is that the private sector, at current costs, cannot provide a supply of new homes to meet the needs of those on modest and above average incomes of between €45,000 and €75,000 even if very significant financial supports were provided by Government in the form of subsidies, tax breaks and reductions in standards.

While the measures introduced to date, and indeed those proposed by the Society of Chartered Surveyors of Ireland, may assist developers in increasing output of homes at the higher price range, it is not clear that they couldn't do this without such supports and it is certainly a questionable use of much-needed tax revenue.

Thus while the overall viability (i.e. profitability) of private sector construction would certainly improve if the Government were to continue with their current trajectory and embrace further subsidies and tax reliefs, the increased supply would not be of the kind that is most urgently needed.

A more sensible approach would be for Government to accept the fact that in current market conditions private developers cannot meet the housing needs of modest and above average income earners and, as outlined in the public housing programme outlined above, invest exchequer revenue in public affordable rental and purchase property.

If public housing was to constitute 50 percent of all new construction, with an annual investment starting at €2.3 billion, this would deliver 15,000 social rental, affordable cost rental and affordable purchase homes which alongside a relatively modest increase in private output would comfortably meet the upper NDP target in advance of 2021. Sinn Féin in their 2019 *Alternative Budget* provided detailed costings demonstrating how this could be achieved.[37]

However, Government should also consider a number of policy interventions to ensure the functioning of the private purchase sector alongside an expanding public house building programme. These interventions should focus of ways of reducing overall development costs without expecting the taxpayer to foot the bill.

In the first instance the proposition that for a development to be viable a developer must receive 11 percent profit on their investment should be challenged. While there is significant risk in development, there are very few other sectors that expect such a high return. If builders (as distinct from developers) operate with profit margins in single digits, there is no reason why developers can't do so. Indeed, there is an argument for Government to focus its support for small and medium sized builders rather than assisting larger scale developers.

For this sector there is a need to address the high cost of land and finance. The issue of land will be dealt with in more detail below. With respect to finance the Government's Home Building Finance Ireland initiative has real potential to assist builders in increasing output. However, as it is currently constituted it runs the risk of repeating the same mistakes as LIHAF by lending to developers who have access to mainstream market finance and not securing an affordability dividend.

The €1.5 billion lending facility (half funded from the Strategic Investment Fund with the remainder secured from private markets) should instead be constructed in a manner not unlike the Rebuilding Roland Home Loan Scheme for first-time buyers. It should provide funding to builders with viable development projects but who are unable to secure sufficient private sector finance. Loans should only be provided in return for the delivery of houses within set price ranges. As the Home Loan product demonstrates, it is possible to apply such constraints on commercial lending without falling foul of EU State Aid rules.

Government should also place a greater emphasis on addressing issues such as the skills shortage through State sponsored apprenticeship programmes and dedicated training centres as well as providing contingency plans to protect building material supply chains to mitigate any negative impacts of Brexit. Both of these areas, rhetoric notwithstanding, have seen little by way of concrete action from Government to date.

Private Purchase Sector Proposal

- Amend the *National Development Plan* targets for private sector commencements to 15,000 per year
- Amend the lending criteria for Home Building Finance Ireland by restricting lending to small and medium sized builders with viable projects who are unable to secure sufficient private bank finance and who commit to affordable house prices
- Develop a Brexit contingency plan for the construction sector focusing on measures to mitigate any negative impact on the supply of building materials or labour
- In conjunction with the Department of Education and Construction Industry Federation introduce a comprehensive apprenticeship and training scheme for the building and associated trades

---

Building Communities, Not Just Homes

Too often public discourse on housing focuses solely on output, on the number, type and location of new housebuilding. It is vital, particularly as output increases, that we remember we are in the process of building communities, not just housing. Issues such as the provision of adequate social and leisure amenities and employment opportunities are central to the success, or indeed failure, of new settlements. Equally, and particularly in public housing estates, issues of maintenance, estate management and tenant participation are vitally important for new communities to succeed.

Despite the fact that these principles are widely accepted in political and policy making circles, residents will often, and with some legitimacy, complain that they are marked more by their omission than their observance.

The issues of maintenance, management and participation in public housing estates came into focus following the 1995 review of *A Plan For Social Housing*. *Social Housing, The Way Ahead*, to its merit, understood the need for better quality management of social housing stock and greater consistency across providers, whether Councils or Approved Housing Bodies.[38] The introduction of Housing Management Initiative Grants and the establishment of a Housing Management Group were all positive out-workings of this new focus.

Enhancing the community function of Local Authority Housing Departments along with the provision of grants for a range of community and estate management activities and dedicated estate management and community staff working on the ground brought significant improvements.

However, the application of this new community orientation in housing policy was often dependent on individual staff and management initiative and lacked a consistency of application across all providers. Resident surveys in both *Social Housing in Ireland* and its 10-year sequel *Social Housing, Disadvantage and Neighbourhood Liveability* highlight criticisms of Councils' response to maintenance, estate management and anti-social behaviour issues in their areas.[39]

There are a number of reasons why the community and estate management functions of housing policy continue to play too peripheral a role in housing practice. The first is the historic relegation of these 'softer' functions when set against the 'serious' business of providing 'bricks and mortar'. Policy priorities, funding allocations and career paths and hierarchies all clearly privileged the provision of homes rather than the sustaining of communities.

There is also a clear power relationship between housing providers and tenants which in the main casts the latter in a passive role, as recipient of a State service rather than an active participant in the shaping of the community in which they live and the policies that govern that estate. Government responses to the tensions that inevitably arose when tenant participation became too independent and too critical of how State agencies responded to communities' needs reinforced these power relationships.

During the 1970s and 1980s in many council estates community-based residents groups emerged to campaign for better services, whether road upgrades and traffic calming, community centres, economic opportunities or measures to address drug addiction and organised crime. Informal campaigns became formal community fora which in turn became the community development sector.

As Government funding became available during the 1990s community-based organisations underwent a period of significant change, increasing their capacity and professionalism and providing much-needed services. At the same time these projects became increasingly dependent on State funding and thus Governmental approval.

The demise of the independent community development sector in the last decade was a result of both funding cuts to and forced amalgamations of community-based groups into more formal and statutory partnership structures. There is no doubt that part of the rationale for these changes was to undermine the sector's independence and critical voice.

Thus at a community level while there is a broader range of facilities and opportunities provided through the community and voluntary sector than was previously the case, the participative connection with the wider community has in many instances been lost.

Local Authorities also experienced significant reductions in staff during the recession due to the public sector recruitment embargo. It is estimated that the Local Government sector lost up to 25 percent of its work force from 2008 to 2014, the biggest percentage loss across the entire State sector. These reductions disproportionately affected the 'soft' or least prioritised functions in such areas as community services and estate management.

The consequence of all of this was that the progress made from the mid-1990s in improving estate management and community functions within public housing estates was at best stalled and at worst undermined and rolled back.

The professionalisation of the community sector also has a consequence in terms of who has access to the available policy-making bodies within Local Government such as the Strategic Policy Committees. Community spaces tend to be allocated to professional community and voluntary sector representatives, which of course is entirely appropriate, but it is not the same as direct resident participation. Again, depending on the Council, more informal mechanisms of direct community engagement can and do happen, but even this is far from ideal.

The post-2014 *Putting People First* Local Government reforms have resulted in some improvements while at the same time reinforcing some of the less positive developments of recent years. The formalisation of the Public Participation Networks has had some benefits though more so for those groups or communities with already higher levels of resourcing and capacity. While the shift of core community sector funding from grant aid to competitive tendering via the Social Inclusion Community Activation Programme has been a retrograde step.

Thus if housing policy is to fully embrace the need for real community participation in improving maintenance services and estate management, and to take on the bigger and ongoing challenge of sustaining vibrant communities, then the tentative changes post-1995 need to be enhanced and mainstreamed. This is particularly necessary in the context of a significant expansion of public sector housing building as argued for here.

To achieve this the first step would be to formally recognise that the 'soft' community and estate management functions are of equal importance to the 'hard' function of building houses. This must be reflected in the staffing and resources given of Local Authorities and community-based projects. It would also require a return to direct grant aid provided to independent Community Development projects, led by local residents and working in partnership with professional community and voluntary sector organisations, Council officials, other statutory providers and elected politicians.

We also need to move beyond a formal culture of community 'consultation' and embrace, resource and realise genuine community 'empowerment' in which the people who live in communities are actively involved in the decisions which affect their lives. This is labour- and resource-intensive.

However, if such an approach had been taken in the expanding public housing sector from the 1970s onwards the capacity of communities to respond effectively to the challenges of the 1980s while holding State agencies to account to ensure they also played their part in addressing problems, would have been considerably greater.

In practical terms this means greater Council investment in creating and sustaining residents associations, tenants fora, and tenant participation in policy formulation and decision-making. The introduction of a pilot Participative Budgeting programme in South Dublin County Council in 2016 is a step in the right direction. However, real participation cannot be reduced to voting for a preferred project in a Local Government version of the X-Factor. Rather it means engaging, educating and empowering communities, particularly those who experience the deepest levels of social and economic marginalisation, to play meaningful policy-formulating and decision-making roles in the lives of their streets, estates and wider communities.

Given the very significant deficit in the quality of many Local Authority maintenance services, often caused by insufficient or badly designed Central Government funding streams, there is a need for Local Authority tenants to have access to the protections of the Residential Tenancies Act and the Residential Tenancies Board, with the exception of the Part IV tenancy regulations, which could be seen as a weakening of existing tenants rights.

Access to the RTB where Councils fail to respond adequately to maintenance requests and cyclical refurbishment would provide a valuable independent check to ensure that Local and Central Government fulfil their landlord responsibilities. Given that the Approved Housing Body sector is already covered by the RTA and RTB it is

---

Community and Estate Management Proposal

- Produce, fund and implement an estate management and resident participation strategy with a clear community development ethos
- End the use of procurement for the provision of Social Inclusion Community Activation Funding and encourage a greater diversity of funding clients rather than the current model of centralised funding for single providers
- Amend the Residential Tenancies Act to ensure that all social rental tenants have the same level of rights and equal access to the Residential Tenancies Board

---

increasingly hard to justify why Local Government housing is not.

Improving Building Control and Consumer Protection

One of the many terrible legacies of the Celtic Tiger housing boom was an as-yet-unknown number of badly built developments and, in particular, apartment complexes. Weak regulation, weaker enforcement and greed on the part of some developers, builders and architects has left thousands of people living in accommodation with significant fire safety and structural defects.

Homes in North County Dublin were built on foundations filled with pyrite, a stone that expands when it comes in contact with moisture, literally tearing homes apart. Pyrite and other defective materials such as mica block were used to construct thousands of homes in Donegal and

Mayo, literally crumbling to pieces when exposed over time to the elements.

Multi-unit developments were built without adequate fire escapes or alarm systems, with no fire stopping to prevent the flood of smoke or fire between units. Water ingress caused by failure to properly construct interfaces between exterior walls and roofs is causing damp, mould and the progressive erosion of the integrity of the buildings.

Priory Hall, a private and affordable housing development in Dublin, was to become the first and most infamous of the latent defects cases. In 2011 serious fire safety and structural defects were discovered in the 180 multi-unit development, leading the fire service to force the evacuation of the entire estate. Following a protracted campaign by homeowners and local politicians the State eventually stepped in and took over the development, spending an estimated €23 million on its refurbishment. While residents were able to walk away debt free, the stress and heartache experienced during the years of campaigning took its toll, including the tragic suicide of 38-year-old homeowner Fiachra Daly in 2013.

The Priory Hall scandal pushed Government into a review of the Building Control legislation that had been in place during the housing boom. The 1990 to 1997 Building Control Acts governed house building and were effectively a form of light-touch self-regulation. Home buyers thought that the fire safety and building compliance certificates that accompanied their homes on purchase meant they had been built according to regulations. However, all they actually meant was that if the property was built in accordance with the plans then it would be compliant.

While rogue developers, builders and architects were principally to blame for Priory Hall and other such developments, the absence of any meaningful inspection and building standards enforcement regime also made the State culpable in the latent defects scandal.

In 2014 the Fine Gael–Labour Government introduced a series of reforms known as the Building Control Amendment Regulations. A new system of professional certification was put in place whereby builders and developers would employ competent professionals to inspect and certify developments at various stages through the process. These would then be lodged onto an online Government Building Control Management System (BCMS). While on-site Local Authority inspection would remain random and not cover all buildings, those in favour of the reform argued that BCMS would allow Council officials to track and red flag developments that may be in breach of the regulations.

Critics of the system argued that it still amounted to self-certification as the certifiers were employed by the builders and developers. They also pointed out potential conflicts of interest as certifiers could be employed in the same company as the architect overseeing the development itself.

Alongside BCR and BCMS Government established a voluntary Construction Industry Register, located in the headquarters of the Construction Industry Federation, the builders and developers principal lobby group. Legislation to put the register on a statutory footing is currently making its way through the Oireachtas.

The Government also introduced a State-funded pyrite remediation scheme to assist some of those whose homes were damaged and are currently considering the introduction of a similar scheme to deal with mica block. However, a more general redress scheme for those left with serious fire safety or water ingress problems is not being considered by Government.

Today there are many housing developments where residents are faced with bills of between €10,000 and €30,000 to remediate properties which they bought in good faith and, through no fault of their own, now require significant structural repair.

In 2016 the Oireachtas Housing Committee agreed to hold a number of hearings on the issue and publish a report with recommendations to Government. *Safe as Houses, A Report on Building Control, Building Standards and Consumer Protection* was published in January 2017 following hearings with and submissions from the Department of Housing, representatives from the construction, certification and fire safety industries, fire safety officials, Local Government planning and Building Control staff, academics and owners of properties with latent defects.

The Committee's work was the first full assessment of the 2014 reforms, albeit after a period of limited new construction. However, given that new build activity was starting to recover, the review was nonetheless timely.

At the core of the Committee's findings was that while the 2014 BCAR and BCMS reforms were an improvement on the previous regime they were not fully independent and needed strengthening. In addition to a more independent Building Control regime the Committee felt that actions in the area of improving building standards, protecting against future defects and addressing the legacy of bad building were also necessary.

The report's recommendations on Building Standards and Consumer Protection included the creation of a new Building Standards and Consumer Protection Agency along the lines of the Food Safety Authority and Environmental Protection Agency. The Agency would not take over the functions of Building Control Authorities but assist them in ensuring greater levels of compliance. It would also support Building Control Agencies in developing and implementing best practice, monitoring and reporting in compliance and enforcement.

The Agency would also have a consumer protection role providing an information, advice, complaints, mediation and dispute resolution service similar to the roles carried out by the Residential Tenancies Board and the Financial Services Ombudsman and provide a fully independent location for the Construction Industry Register.

Not unlike the Housing Agency the new body could also assist Government and industry with policy development, research and data collection while fulfilling the role of construction qualifications registration authority and custodian of the Building Control Management System.

In order to make the Building Control system truly independent the Committee recommended breaking the self-certification element of the 2014 reforms by having Local Authorities employ the assigned certifiers, either on a contract basis or as full-time local authority employees. The costs of certification would remain with the developer/ builder who would pay Local Authorities directly in respect of fees with no additional handling fee being levied by the local authority.

Neither Design Certifiers nor Assigned Certifiers could be employed by a developer/builder on either the project they are certifying or any other project with that developer in any other role. Local Authorities would also not be allowed to self-certify or employ assigned certifiers for their own social housing developments. This would be contracted out via the Building Standards and Consumer Protection Agency.

The Committee also felt that fire safety inspections by specialist Building Control officers should be mandatory for all multiple occupancy developments or developments with a higher level of fire risk. Such inspections should be required prior to the submission of a Completion Certificate and no building could be opened, used or occupied without a completion certificate being issued.

With respect to protection for future home buyers the Committee recommended that latent defects insurance should be a legal requirement to be provided by the developer/builder on the sale of all new residential properties. In addition the report called for a series of legal reforms including transmissible warranties of quality from developers/builders and those involved in the building process in favour of first and subsequent purchasers, and a new statute of limitations of two years from discovery of defect rather than six years from purchase of the property.

The Committee also felt strongly that there should be a bar on the awarding of public contracts to developers/ builders or associated construction professionals found to have been in serious breach of building standards or fire safety regulations.

Finally, *Safe as Houses* recommended that Government should establish a redress scheme to assist homeowners with latent defects. The mission statement of the redress scheme should be: 'Ordinary owners who purchased in good faith should not be liable for the costs of remediation caused by the incompetence, negligence or deliberate non-compliance of others.'

The scheme should provide an information and advice service for those affected by non-compliance and regulatory failure as well as a remediation fund to cover the costs of works where the original builder or developer was no longer trading. While not being prescriptive as to how the fund should be resourced the Committee urged Government to look at options including an industry levy matched by Government funding, allowing homeowners to write off the costs of remedial works against their tax liabilities, and an interest-free loan scheme to assist homeowners in funding the cost of remedial works.

In order to fully establish the scale of the latent defects issue the Committee also recommended that there should be a programme of fire risk assessments based on a methodology designed to assess those boom-time developments deemed potentially at risk of containing latent defects.

The *Safe as Houses* report received a mixed response, warmly welcomed by homeowners with latent defects and supported by academics and some professionals. However, Department of Housing officials, some Local Government planning staff and representatives of both the construction and architecture professions were highly critical.

Nevertheless, if we are to ensure that the construction industry is never again allowed to repeat the scandals of the 1990s and 2000s then we need a more robust Building Control system, fully independent of industry and with strong consumer protections. We also need to ensure that those left in structurally unsound properties built during the last housing boom are not left to carry the cost for remediation of defects which they did not cause. The recommendations of the Oireachtas Housing Committee report are, to date, the best set of proposals to achieve these objectives.

> **Building Standards Proposal**
>
> • Fully implement the 26 recommendations of the Oireachtas Housing Committee *Safe as Houses* report

Planning for the Future

Concerns about the inappropriate relationships between politicians and developers has been a feature of the housing system since the start of the twentieth century. However, widespread planning and zoning corruption was confirmed following the publication of the final Mahon Tribunal report in 2012. The five-year long tribunal into certain planning matters and payments examined, over nine modules, allegations of politicians accepting payments in exchange for rezoning of lands and assistance with other planning matters. The final report was a damning indictment of a regime then in existence in Dublin Corporation in which a nexus of corruption involved land owners, property developers, estate agents, lobbyists and Local and Central Government politicians, including Ministers.

In addition to corruption, the Mahon Tribunal exposed a weak regulatory system for planning which resulted in decisions being made with long-term negative impacts for thousands of people. The decision to abandon the long-standing plan for a town centre between Clondalkin and Lucan on the Clonburris lands in West Dublin in favour of an out-of-town retail park in the nearby Quarryvale site is a case in point. Instead of the residents of the expanding Dublin suburb getting a proper civic and social centre with public services, employment opportunities and appropriate retail it became the location for the first motorway-based retail park designed to meet the needs of commuters rather than the local community.[40]

Of course, not all bad planning decisions were the result of politicians taking bribes from developers. During the Celtic Tiger under-funded Councils were incentivised to approve developments in order to secure development levies to fund much-needed services. In some of the most extreme cases permission was granted to build on flood planes with disastrous consequences for homeowners.

Judge Mahon, in his final report, made a wide-ranging series of recommendations for reform of planning law, regulation of conflicts of interest in political decision-making and transparency and anti-corruption law. Many of his recommendations were introduced, however others remain outstanding.

Most recently his proposal for the establishment of an independent planning regulator was significantly watered down in legislation passed by the Oireachtas in 2018. Judge Mahon criticised the 'over-centralisation of power in the hands of the Minister' for Environment and recommended that 'the Minister's ... ability to give directions to Regional Authorities and Local Planning Authorities should be entrusted to a Planning Regulator'.

The Planning and Development (Amendment) Act 2018 puts in place a regulator appointed by the Minister with powers to investigate but only recommend action to the Minister. Instead of addressing the 'over-centralisation of power' in the heads of the Minister and Department, the legislation has actually increased that power. With the first Planning Regulator appointed in December 2018 it is too early to tell what impact the new office will have on the planning regime.

More broadly, housing policy became increasingly focused on issues of planning and the need for greater coordination between Central, Regional and Local Government plans. The Planning and Development Act 2000 obliged Local Authorities to develop six-year development plans to better coordinate all aspects of their administrative areas' development, including proper zoning and planning.

The 2000 Act also introduced the regulations governing Strategic Development Zones which were an attempt both to allow for more integrated master-planning of large, important public and private land banks while at the same time streamlining and fast-tracking the planning and decision-making – two objectives that do not always sit easily together.

The most notable Strategic Development Zones have been those in Dublin's Docklands and Adamstown in the west of the city. While the former has been heavily criticised for its social cleansing of the local working-class communities surrounding Sheriff Street to make way for more upmarket residential development, the latter has emerged, recession delays notwithstanding, as an example of better planning and more integrated residential and social-economic development.

While the creation of Regional Plans and in 2002 the first National Spatial Strategy attempted to put these local plans in a broader context, their non-statutory footing was identified by the 2004 NESC *Housing in Ireland* reports as a significant weakness. This, combined with heavily politicised policy decisions by Government, such as the infamous and ultimately unsuccessful decentralisation plan introduced by Finance Minister Charlie McCreevy in the mid-2000s, meant that much of the National Spatial Strategy remained unachieved.

More recently the placing of an updated National Planning Framework on a statutory footing is an attempt to resolve many of the issues identified by both NESC and policy commitments included in the 2007 *Delivering Homes, Sustaining Communities*. The plan has significant weaknesses, particularly in relation to the spatial distribution of socio-economic disadvantage and proper all-Ireland planning integration. It also lacks ambition in meeting the challenge of climate change as a result of its modest commitments to improve public transport provision and increase renewable energy output.

Nevertheless, the existence of a statutory plan, and the improved public consultation in its development are all steps in the right direction.

At the core of all of the developments since 2000 have been an intersecting set of planning concerns. Locally the challenge has been how to ensure that residential settlements are developed in a planned and coordinated manner with social and economic infrastructure including transport, educational and community facilities and economic opportunity. More broadly the focus has been on how to reverse the depopulation of our city and town centres while limiting suburban sprawl and unrestricted one-off rural housing.

These objectives have been set in the context of ensuring better regional balance statewide, reversing the unsustainable trend of overdevelopment of Dublin and its immediate commuter belt, and revitalising the State's other main population centres such as Cork and Galway while supporting rural communities and promoting North–South integration particularly along the border region and in the north-west.

Ultimately planning policy and national or regional plans remain aspirational if not adequately supported by sustained investment. Opposition politicians were strongly critical of the mismatch between the commitments as set out in the National Planning Framework on the one hand and the low levels of investment, particularly in the initial years, in the accompanying *National Development Plan.*

The fact that neither were subject to formal Oireachtas approval, despite the legislation underpinning the National Planning Framework clearly requiring a vote, reflects the Government's fear of not being able to secure its passage due to objections.

Opposition politicians and indeed many in the planning community have also expressed concern at interventions by successive Ministers, such as Alan Kelly's 2016 regulations and Eoghan Murphy's 2018 regulations on apartment building and Simon Coveney's 2017 fast-track planning.

Minister Coveney was correct in seeking to reduce the length of time it took for large-scale residential developments to pass through the planning process. However, his Strategic Housing Development legislation was the least democratic way of doing this. Rather than place clear statutory time frames for pre-planning, additional information requests and appeals, which would have reduced the planning time frame, the Minister chose to bypass Local Authorities and the local democratic process in order to 'avoid the eccentricities' of the City and County Development Plans, as one senior Department of Housing official explained to me off the record. While a small number of large developers were pleased with the outcome, the planning process was much the poorer for it.

While there is broad agreement of the need to increase the population densities within the canals in Dublin City, both Ministers' actions actively undermined the democratically agreed City Development Plan.

Planning Proposals

- Fully implement all of the Mahon Tribunal planning recommendations including a fully independent Planning Regulator
- Bring forward review of the NPF to 2021, expand the public consultation process and ensure the revised plan is subject to Oireachtas approval
- Reverse the planning changes introduced by Ministers Kelly, Coveney and Murphy since 2016 and replace them with a statewide strategy for densification of the urban cores of Dublin, Cork and other cities as appropriate following adequate consultation with Local Authorities, planning professionals and other stakeholders

---

These changes fly in the face of policy recommendations made by independent bodies such as NESC and reflect more the demands of certain institutional investors rather than the requirements of proper planning and spatial development.

Managing Land for the Common Good

The issue of land, land values and speculative investment has been at the centre of housing policy anxieties since the late 1960s. While many commentators view land as just another factor of production, a cost in house building just like labour or materials, the reality is very different.

As Ryan-Collins, Lloyd and Macfarlane highlight in their ground-breaking book *Rethinking the Economics of Land and Housing*, land is a factor of production unlike any other. The finite and ever reducing availability of land gives it a very different character to other ingredients of residential development which have been ignored by economists and housing policy specialists. It has become, particularly since the liberalisation of bank and mortgage finance since the 1980s, the preferred object of investment, leading to ever greater increases in value, in turn driving up house prices and rents.

Indeed, this preference for investment in land as a more secure asset due to its recoverability in case of default, has meant the balance of institutional investment has shifted dramatically across much of the OECD from the productive economy to land speculation, with much broader impacts on job creation and economic development. In turn, ever greater levels of mortgage finance and equity withdrawal have pushed household debt to historic highs, again with significant impacts on the stability of the broader economy.

What to do about the interaction between speculative investment in land and the affordability of housing has been a periodic concern for successive Irish Governments. The 1972 *Report from the Committee on the Price of Land*, known generally as the Kenny report after its principal author John Kenny, was the first in a series of Government commissioned enquiries, followed by the *Report of the Joint Oireachtas Committee on Building Land* in 1986, the *Ninth Progress Report of the All-Party Oireachtas Committee on the Constitution* dealing with private property in 2000 and the National Economic and Social Council *Urban Development Land* report in 2018.

The report's proposal for a Designated Areas Scheme through which Compulsory Purchase Orders would be used to acquire land at its existing use value plus 25 percent still has merit today. While opponents will continue to cite the constitutional protection of private property, as the report rightly highlights these can be constrained in the interests of the common good and in accordance with principles of social justice.

Indeed, recent Supreme Court rulings, such as that on the Part V provisions of the Planning and Development Act of 2000, clearly indicate the scope for State intervention to protect the common good. The judgement is worth quoting at length:

> In the present case, as a condition of obtaining a planning permission for the development of lands for residential purposes, the owner may be required to cede some part of the enhanced value of the land deriving both from its zoning for residential purposes and the grant of permission in order to meet what is considered by the Oireachtas to be a desirable social objective, namely the provision of affordable housing and housing for persons in the special categories and of integrated housing. Applying the tests proposed by Costello J. in Heaney v. Ireland [1994] 3 I.R. 593 and subsequently endorsed by this court, the court in the case of the present Bill is satisfied that the scheme passes those tests. They are rationally connected to an objective of sufficient importance to warrant interference with a constitutionally protected right and, given the serious social problems which they are designed to meet, they undoubtedly relate to concerns which, in a free and democratic society, should be regarded as pressing and substantial. At the same time, the court is satisfied that they impair those rights as little as possible and their effects on those

rights are proportionate to the objectives sought to be attained.[41]

The key issue is not whether the State can interfere in private property rights, by compulsorily acquiring land at below market prices to meet social and affordable housing need, but whether specific interventions are justified and appropriate compensation provided.

The Society of Chartered Surveyors of Ireland's reports cited earlier shows that the land element of housing prices is significant and rising. In a more extreme example a developer in a Dublin suburb was claiming that the land value on each apartment in a specific development in 2017 was €98,000 and that was at the discounted existing land use value as part of a Part V purchase by Dún Laoghaire–Rathdown County Council.[42]

In the same year the State broadcaster RTÉ sold 8.5 acres of its Montrose studio site for a record price of €107.5 million, €25.5 million above the guide price. With a plan to build 500 apartments on the site this would mean that the land value per apartment was an astonishing €210,000.

In addition to the impact of speculative investment, fuelled by the multi-billion euro wall of money discussed above, the completely unregulated and opaque nature of the market in land and the reality of land hoarding by certain developers despite having both active planning permission and sufficient funds to develop, makes understanding the full impact of land on affordable housing supply difficult to fully understand and evidence.

Alongside this, since the NESC 2004 *Housing in Ireland* report there have been repeated calls for a more active land management policy to be formulated by Government.

Part of the demand is for Government to make better strategic use of all public land holdings, including those held by semi-State companies. This has been accompanied by proposals to leverage public land to unlock residential development and make better use of compulsory purchase orders in locations of high land values in order to temper the market.

The creation of the Land Development Agency in 2018 will facilitate some of these functions, though the full extent of its impact will not be known until both its statutory underpinning and ultimate budget are revealed later in 2019. However as highlighted earlier, the development framework included in the LDA's remit – insisting that 60 percent of homes on its land will be sold at open market prices by private developers as part of an off-balance sheet joint venture model – will dramatically undermine its strategic function in terms of meeting social and affordable housing need.

What is needed is a much more ambitious programme of land policy reform. At the centre of this must be a policy of actively increasing the stock of publicly owned land, whether for residential or commercial use. In order for this to be financially viable some form of legal restrictions on the price paid during the compulsory purchase process will be required, whether in the form of the 1972 Land Report recommendations or in some updated form.

There is also a need to revisit the financial liberalisation of the 1980s and 1990s. As discussed earlier, there is clear evidence of the negative impact on housing affordability caused by the lifting of various credit restrictions during these decades. There is merit in considering the reintroduction of credit controls in their original or more updated form alongside a return to a more localised relationship banking model as argued for by Ryan-Collins, Lloyd and Macfarlane.[43]

Alongside this, simple measures such as a live land market registry recording in real time the price paid for land on the open market would create greater transparency and assist Government in establishing exactly where the greatest pressures lie and where intervention is most needed.

There is also a need to revisit the issue of taxation of land, no matter how politically contentious the issue may be. The current vacant site tax is widely seen as ineffective and is urgently in need of review. The low number of sites on Local Authority vacant sites registers and the low level of the tax applied – just 3 percent from 2019 – are clear evidence that it is not designed to do what is required, disincentivise land hoarding and speculative investment.

In addition to strengthening the powers and ability of Councils to place all vacant sites on their register, the tax must be increased to a level that is genuinely punitive. Independent Deputy Mick Wallace introduced the Urban Regeneration and Housing (Amendment) Bill 2018 to achieve exactly this objective, hiking the vacant site levy to 25 percent.[44] The Bill was opposed by both Fine Gael and Fianna Fáil.

There is also a need for a broader review of both the way in which land speculation is financed and taxed, to consider a range of possible measures that could, in perpetuity, end the corrosive impact of speculative investment in land on the housing system. This could be done as part of a broader review of land policy in the form of an updated Kenny report, produced with very focused terms of reference to recommend measures to address land

---

Land Reform

- Introduce a Designated Area Scheme based on the 1972 Kenny report but updated following consultation with legal and planning experts
- Legislate for a real time land market registry to provide transparency in the market for land
- Reform the Vacant Sites Levy by raising the level of tax to a genuinely punitive level and removing the exemptions
- Review the broader tax treatment of land and regulation of bank lending for land purchase with a view to macro-prudential rules to dampen the speculative market in land
- Amend Land Development Agency legislation to ensure that where residential development takes place it is done in the context of prioritising the provision of public housing to meet social and affordable need

---

speculation and price inflation, to be produced within a very limited timeframe of no more than a year.

Meeting the Challenge of Climate Change

It will come as no surprise that *Delivering Homes, Sustaining Communities* and *Social Housing Strategy 2020* failed to mention the issue of climate change and the role residential developments play in carbon emissions. However, the failure of *Rebuilding Ireland* to make any reference to reducing carbon emissions from residential development is a surprise, given the Government requirement to meet the EU Near Zero Energy Regulations in all new public buildings by 2018 and all buildings by 2020.

Residential and commercial buildings account for 40 percent of energy consumption and 36 percent of CO_2 emissions across the European Union. In Ireland the energy consumption level is closer to 30 percent as is CO_2 emission level. However, Irish homes emit almost 60 percent more CO_2 than the EU average. Clearly we can only meet our climate change targets if the levels of carbon-related energy consumption are reduced dramatically in the coming years.

A recently published NGO Climate Change Performance Index ranked Ireland 45th out of 57 countries on greenhouse gas emissions, renewable energy, and energy use. The Germanwatch, NewClimate Institute and Climate Action Network Europe report categorised Ireland as a 'Very Low performing' country – the worst ranking available.[45]

While the report didn't come as a surprise it is the latest in a long line of wake-up calls to both the Government and society more generally that we are not taking the issue of climate change seriously. Given the high levels of energy consumption that occur within homes the need for Government to ensure that we meet both our 2018 and 2020 nZEB (nearly Zero Energy Building) obligations is essential.

The absence of any serious discussion of the implications of climate change mitigation for housing policy is a failing that cannot be allowed to continue. While discussion of how to meet the nZEB requirements has preoccupied technical specialists in planning departments and building practice, it has not yet become a mainstream component of our policy debate.

Government transposed the Energy Performance of Buildings Directive into planning law in January 2017 and provided industry with accompanying guidance in the form of Technical Guidance Document L. According to Government the directive defines a Nearly Zero Energy Building as a building that has a very high energy performance and that the nearly zero or very low amount of energy required should be covered to a very significant extent by energy from renewable sources, including energy from renewable sources produced on-site or nearby. Typically such buildings would have a BER A2 rating. However, despite a number of Parliamentary Questions to both the Minister for Climate Action and the Minister for Housing in early January, it is not yet clear whether the State has met its 2018 obligations under the directive.[46] While both Ministers confirmed that 98 percent of new buildings now have a BER A3 rating, they could not confirm the number that were reaching the nZEB requirement of A2.

However, while progress is being made in terms of new builds there are very significant numbers of older buildings, including those built between 2000 and 2014, with very low levels of energy efficiency. The latest figures from the CSO are set out it the table below.[47]

Since its establishment the Sustainable Energy Authority of Ireland (SEAI) provided grant aid to 375,000 households to upgrade their energy performance. Nevertheless, the overall volume of grant aid and the design of the schemes have meant that take up is nowhere near the level needed. This is particularly the case in the private rental sector where 55 percent of buildings have a BER rating of D or less.

The public housing sector is just as bad with 50 percent of all social housing having an energy rating of D or less. However, incremental increases in grant aid for energy

BER Ratings by Period of Construction

Period of construction	% of row						
	Energy rating						
	A	B	C	D	E	F-G	Total
1700–1977	0	4	18	25	20	33	245,143
1978–1999	0	5	40	36	13	6	233,323
2000–2004	0	9	60	22	6	2	145,725
2005–2009	1	35	51	10	3	1	138,375
2010–2014	36	55	7	1	0	0	10,793
2015–2018	97	3	0	0	0	0	29,214

improvement schemes have seen retrofitting of 64,000 units and 9,000 voids in recent years.

Not only does the low energy efficiency of social and private rental stock contribute to CO_2 emissions and climate change, it is also one of the major causes of fuel poverty. The State has the fourth highest electricity prices in the EU and almost 400,000 households in fuel poverty.

Under the *National Development Plan,* Government plans to increase the number of households availing of retrofitting grants from the SEAI to 45,000 per year. However, many believe both the number and the depth of the retrofits is not sufficient.

There is a need for a much more ambitious programme of deep retrofitting. This should target the 21 percent of homes that use solid fuel or have no central heating and the 47 percent of households that use oil, as this fuel emits 50 percent more carbon than gas.

There has been some discussion about striking the right balance between greater use of renewable energy sources and reductions in overall energy consumption through the adoption of the Passive House Standard. The difficulties in storing renewable energy at a domestic level and the lack of networked renewables makes this an even more pressing question.

In 2018 the Citizens Assembly, modelled on the Constitutional Convention but examining broader policy issues, examined how the State could become a leader in tackling climate change. The Third Assembly Report published in April 2018 recommended that

> All new buildings should have a zero or low carbon footprint and planning permission should only be granted for new builds which comply with these requirements. The Government should provide incentives to retrofit homes to achieve better energy efficiency ratings.[48]

While both the nZEB planning requirements and the SEAI and Local Authority retrofitting programmes are in line with this recommendation the real question is whether sufficient investment, monitoring and enforcement will be forthcoming.

To date the low levels of investment in retrofitting of public and private buildings and the absence of any clear monitoring or enforcement of the 2018 and 2020 nZEB targets confirms that just as with other areas of public policy, in housing the Government has yet to demonstrate the required level of urgency in tackling the threat of climate change.

Sustainability Proposals

- Publish a comprehensive strategy to reduce the carbon emissions from all residential dwellings including increased investment in deep retrofitting of public and private homes, monitoring and enforcement of the 2018 and 2020 nZEB requirements
- Ensure adequate funding from Central and Local Government to underpin all of the commitments in the strategy
- Set more ambitious NDP targets for deep retrofitting of public and private buildings

---

Ending Housing Inequality

While under-provision of public housing coupled with the vagaries of the private market have left many individual households without adequate housing, there are specific groups in society which have been disproportionately disadvantaged as a result of institutionalised discrimination, poor policy decisions or failure to understand how our dysfunctional housing system can place barriers in the way of specific groups of people accessing secure and affordable accommodation.

Travellers, people with disabilities, those experiencing homelessness, migrants and asylum seekers all face specific structural barriers to adequate housing which are the direct results of action and inactions of successive Governments. It is important that in the context of a new approach to public housing provision that sets out to meet the housing needs of the many and not just the few, those groups least served by traditional policy approaches are identified and the barriers removed from the outset so that our more functional housing system does not replicate the inequalities of its predecessors.

The Commission on Itineracy in 1963 sought to eradicate the nomadic culture of Travellers by forcing them into settled housing. The move failed and simply forced Travellers into illegal occupation of roadside camps.

It took more than twenty years for a change of mindset in our political system. The 1995 *Task Force on the Travelling People* finally acknowledged that public policy should support Traveller culture. It was followed in 1998 by the Housing (Traveller Accommodation) Act.

Local Authorities now had a statutory responsibility to meet the needs of the Travelling community. They had to set up Local Traveller Accommodation Consultative Committees and produce five-year Traveller Accommodation Plans which would be funded by a dedicated departmental budget.

While these were very positive moves, an independent report commissioned by the Department of Housing and published in June 2017 highlighted significant problems with the implementation of the programmes over twenty years.

Over the four programmes there was a total allocation of €355.7 million of which 13 percent was unspent. However, the programmes failed to meet their targets for new accommodation by 31 percent, providing just 6,394 of the 9,390 units promised.

Unlike other Government funding streams the programme underspend increased with time. The 2000–2004 programme overspent by 6 percent while the three subsequent programmes underspent by 16 percecnt, 29 percent and 39 percent respectively. Worse still, the underspend hit 45 percent in 2017 and 44 percent in 2018.

While some Local Authorities meet and even exceed their targets others repeatedly missed theirs.

The Minister of State with responsibility for Traveller Accommodation Damien English has convened an Expert Group to make recommendations on how best to address the problems.

Speaking to the Oireachtas Housing Committee on 6 November 2018 Expert Group member Professor Michelle Norris said that the Traveller accommodation issue was solvable as the numbers were low, legislation was good and funding was available. She said the key problem was implementation and barriers to getting projects off the ground.[49] The group will report back later this year.

Their recommendations will provide an opportunity to fix the problems in delivering Traveller accommodation in advance of the next five-year programme. But that will require some radical action including taking planning and land disposal powers away from Councils who refuse to fulfil their legal responsibilities. That will take political courage on behalf of the Minister, his Cabinet colleagues and the Dáil.

According to the Disability Federation of Ireland there are over 4,000 households on Local Authority housing waiting lists with one or more household members with an enduring physical, sensory, mental health or intellectual disability. There are also 1,000 people with disabilities under the age of sixty-five living inappropriately in nursing homes for older people and 2,580 disabled people still living in congregated settings, often called 'institutions', at the end of 2016.

According to the *Discrimination and Inequality in Housing* report published in 2018 by the Human Rights and Equality Commission and the Economic and Social Research

Institute, people with a disability 'are more than twice as likely as people without a disability to report discrimination in access to housing'. They went on to say that

> Moreover, they are 1.6 times more likely than non-disabled people to live in a neighbourhood with environmental problems and 1.6 times more likely to suffer from housing deprivation. In addition, while people with a disability represent about 13 per cent of the Irish population, they make up 27 per cent of homeless people. Again the consistency of evidence from different sources and the persistence of housing disadvantage net of geographical location, income and housing tenure suggests that the disabled group face additional exclusionary forces, including discrimination.[50]

Government policy with respect to the housing needs of people with disabilities is set out in the *National Housing Strategy 2011–2016* and the subsequent implementation reports. In the main the focus is on coordination between service providers and State agencies alongside limited funding for new housing and adaptations.

While there is a clear argument for increasing both of these funding allocations the Oireachtas Disability Group has urged Government to go further and 'Commit 7 percent of all social housing stock in 2019 to the provision of appropriate housing for people with disabilities, provided through both new build and acquisition'.

There is also a need for greater use of universal design for all public and private residential dwellings to ensure an adequate supply of appropriate and accessible accommodation into the future.

Homelessness is the most obvious example of housing inequality. It is caused by the failure of the housing system to meet the needs of specific groups of people who due to various factors are denied access to any form of housing at all. While homelessness is often most common among people with complex needs including addiction, mental ill-health, or a history of institutionalisation these are not causes of homelessness. It is the inability of the housing system to meet these people's needs which is at issue.

Fianna Fáil, when last in Government, published *Homeless, An Integrated Strategy* in 2000. The focus of the strategy was to improve the quality and consistency of responses to homelessness. This was followed by *The Way Ahead, A Plan to Address Adult Homelessness* in 2008 which set 2010 as a target for ending long-term homelessness and the need to sleep rough. At that time there were approximately 1,394 people in emergency accommodation.

Needless to say the 2010 deadline wasn't met, nor as detailed earlier was the subsequent 2016 deadline as committed to in the Government's homeless policy of 2011. Rather homelessness, and increasingly family homelessness, has risen dramatically.

The consistent under-provision of social housing and over-reliance on subsidised private rental tenancies to meet social housing need was badly exposed when in 2014 dramatically rising rents pushed increasing numbers of families into emergency accommodation.

With a more than 300 percent increase in family and child homelessness since 2014, service providers have struggled to provide adequate emergency accommodation for those in need. Meanwhile Government policy has failed to take the necessary measures to stem the flow of families into homelessness or move those in emergency accommodation on to permanent housing quickly enough.

The result has been a homeless crisis of previously unseen proportions as up to 13,000 adults and children are in emergency accommodation or sleep rough with an even greater unknown number sofa surfing or living in chronically overcrowded accommodation. Government policy has become increasingly reactive yet too slow to reverse the trend of growing need.

There is an urgent need for a new homelessness plan which both sets a firm and realistic date for ending long-term homelessness and the need to sleep rough, while at the same time implementing emergency measures to reduce both new homelessness and the length of time people spend in emergency accommodation.

As with Travellers, those with disabilities and those experiencing homelessness, non-Irish nationals experience significant problems in the housing market. The Human Rights and Equality Commission report confirmed this when they reported that

> The Black ethnic group are 3.5 times more likely than White Irish people to experience discrimination, and are significantly over-represented among homeless people (together with Travellers). Ethnicity is not available in the SILC data used to study housing and neighbourhood quality, so here we examine differences in experiences by nationality. In fact, there is a strong overlap between ethnicity and nationality; according to the QNHS, 89 per cent of Black people in Ireland come from outside the EU. Migrants from outside the EU are 2.5 times more likely than Irish nationals to live in over-crowded households.[51]

The situation for those seeking asylum and indeed for those who have been granted their legal leave to remain but are unable to exit Direct Provision is even worse. Introduced in 2001 Direct Provision is a form of institutionalised living where those seeking asylum live in cramped conditions in commercial hotels and other premises managed by private companies in service legal agreements with the Department of Justice. The system is designed to keep asylum seekers segregated from the wider community. It has been regularly subjected to criticism for the poor quality of the housing and food.

Not only are there significant human rights concerns regarding the treatment of residents in Direct Provision, but it has also cost the State €1.25 billion since it was introduced. Given that there are on average 3,000 asylum seekers in the system at any one time a more human rights-compliant reception accommodation system in which all individuals and families have own door accommodation would not only be cheaper it would also allow those fleeing war and persecution the opportunity to live in dignity while their asylum application is being processed.

A truly functional housing system will be judged not just by how it treats the general population but crucially on how it treats those who are most vulnerable or those who traditionally have been most excluded from secure and affordable accommodation.

Ensuring that Travellers, people with disabilities, those experiencing homelessness, migrants and those seeking asylum have access to appropriate, secure and affordable accommodation will be the ultimate test of whether our housing system is really and truly functioning.

Tackling Housing Inequality

- Increase the Traveller Accommodation budget to €40 million, ensure through Ministerial intervention that budget allocations are spent by Local Authorities and ensure that the recommendations of the Expert Group on Traveller accommodation are fully implemented
- Set a new and realistic date for the ending of long-term homelessness and the need to sleep rough and adequately resource Housing First and other public housing solutions to ensure that no person or family is in emergency accommodation for more than six months
- Introduce emergency legislation to stem the flow of individuals and families into homelessness including changes to section 34 of the Residential Tenancies Act and a moratorium on evictions into homelessness
- Publish new housing strategies for people with disabilities and for the new Irish communities, following consultation with relevant stakeholders, to remove barriers experienced by these communities in accessing appropriate, secure and affordable accommodation
- Replace the system of privately contracting out Direct Provision accommodation for those in the asylum process and replace it with Approved Housing Body and NGO led provision of own door accommodation

Conclusion

There is no quick fix to replacing our dysfunctional housing system. It will take time, substantial investment and radical policy change. The programme outlined above offers a pathway to a housing system that can meet the needs of all those unable to access secure and affordable housing in the market or in market housing but with real affordability issues.

Underpinning housing policy with a human rights-based approach is key but also requires substantial investment in public housing to meet social and affordable housing need. Better regulation of both the private rental and purchase sectors is also needed to ensure stability and quality. However, in our drive to meet housing need we must ensure that building standards, proper planning and community viability are not sacrificed. We must also ensure that housing inequality is tackled while at the same time rising to the challenge of climate change by improving our energy efficiency and reducing CO_2 emissions.

These things can all be achieved. Housing systems can and do change. Our own history tells us that. However, the first step in making this happen is to understand the structural causes of our dysfunctional housing system in order to start to put in place alternative policies, investment strategies and regulations that can remove the causes of housing need in order to build a system that functions in the interests of the many and not just the few.

Coda

It's Time to Raise the Roof

Rebuilding Ireland, the Government's housing plan, is not working. In January 2019 Brendan Kenny, the Director of Housing in Dublin City Council, said that it would take years to tackle the housing crisis. He told *The Times* newspaper that it would be 'three years before there is any real difference' in the capital's housing situation.[1] For the lead housing official in the State's largest Local Authority to say that Government housing policy would only start to make a difference a year after their six-year plan expires is, whether intentionally or not, a clear admission of failure.

In my opinion the suggestion that progress will be in evidence in the coming years is wistfully optimistic. While *Rebuilding Ireland* may take the harshest edges off the current housing emergency, and even that is not guaranteed, it cannot deal with the underlying causes of our dysfunctional housing system. At best it will leave us in the same position we were in pre-crash in terms of the need for social and affordable housing and levels of homelessness.

The reason *Rebuilding Ireland* is not working is because it is based on the same flawed policy consensus that has dominated Government thinking and action on housing since the late 1980s. An under-provision of public housing, an over-reliance on the private sector to meet social and affordable housing need, a privileging of owner-occupation, and an under-regulation of the private rental and purchase sectors, all of which combined generate significant structural inequalities in our housing system alongside huge unmet social housing need and recurring rental and purchase affordability crises.

So just as *A Plan for Social Housing* didn't work and *Delivering Homes, Sustaining Communities* didn't work and the *Social Housing Strategy 2020* didn't work, nor can *Rebuilding Ireland*.

This is no longer just the view of those of us on the opposition benches in the Oireachtas or of critical voices in the non-governmental or academic sectors. A growing number of people, directly and indirectly affected by the failure of Government housing policy, clearly agree.

A RedC opinion poll carried out for the *Sunday Business Post* in October 2018 showed that 73 percent of respondents did not believe that Budget 2019 did enough to tackle the housing crisis.[2] Significantly the number of Fine Gael and Fianna Fáil voters who shared this view was 67 percent and 74 percent respectively. A clear majority of voters of both parties did not accept their preferred politicians' claim that Fine Gael and Fianna Fáil had delivered a housing budget.

In January 2019 *The Irish Daily Mail* published an 'Ireland Thinks' poll which stated that 44 percent of respondents placed housing as the issue of most importance to them. Not only was housing at the top of people's agenda, but it was also almost four times more important than Brexit or the crises in health services.[3]

Housing is the social policy issue of our time. It is at the very epicentre of our political debate and exercising an ever greater number of people than at any other time in recent history.

Of course, housing systems do not change by themselves. And while Fine Gael and Fianna Fáil TDs and Senators will come under increasing pressure from their constituents to do more to address housing need, this in and of itself will not force any significant policy change.

What history does tell us, however, is that real systemic change is only brought about when popular mobilisation combined with progressive parliamentary action either forces those in positions of power to change course or removes them from power and replaces them with others willing to make the changes they refused to countenance.

All of the progressive changes in housing policy since the end of the nineteenth century, whether large or small, were the direct result of popular mobilisation and progressive institutional action. The Land League to abolish rural landlordism, Trade Union mobilisations to clear the slums and provide homes for working people, the Housing Action groups in the 1960s and 1970s demanding better quality housing for all are all evidence that popular mobilisation and progressive parliamentary action can deliver real change.

David Clapham, one of the world's leading housing policy experts, argues that change in housing systems is invariably 'slow and gradual because of the inertia and vested interests of the institutions within it'. However, he also argues that 'there are certain critical junctures at which governments choose particular paths and where radical change may take place'. He asks whether we are now at a 'critical juncture in many countries' and suggests that

Certainly, there is a growing disquiet in many places about the direction of current policies and the 'monstrous hybrid' that neoliberalism has left behind, and that has contributed to the seemingly intractable growth of problems such as homelessness. The Global Financial Crisis of 2008 has highlighted pressing problems in many countries and the seeming inability or unwillingness of national governments to deal with them.[4]

Ten years on from the crash and this inability or unwillingness of successive Irish Governments to deal with their dysfunctional housing system has generated a level of anger not seen before. In 2018 we witnessed a significant increase in popular mobilisation and progressive institutional action on the housing front.

The Housing and Homeless Coalition demonstration in Dublin in April of that year and the Take Back the City occupations in August and September were all accompanied by motions and opposition Private Members Bills in City and County Councils and the Oireachtas seeking increased investment in public housing and radical policy change to tackle the housing and homeless crises.

The Raise the Roof initiative, launched in September and led by the Irish Congress of Trade Unions, and its successful 3 October mobilisation and cross-party housing motion brought the housing campaign to a new level. This was echoed weeks later in the 1 December Housing and Homeless Coalition rally, again in Dublin.

On 24 January 2019 Raise The Roof launched a major campaign focused on securing a significant programme of public housing construction, action on rents and tenant security and the creation of a new, legal right to housing.

The campaign will include conferences discussing policy alternatives, a statewide petition to build public support for a legal right to housing, a series of regional rallies and lobbying of Local Authorities on delivery of public housing, along with the holding of a major statewide demonstration later in 2019.

Speaking at the launch, Sheila Nunan, President of the Irish Congress of Trade Unions, said:

> This week marks the centenary of the First Dail and the Democratic Programme, which demanded that private property rights be 'subordinated' to wider public welfare. Today's housing emergency graphically illustrates the failure to do so. Last October, with support from Raise the Roof in the form of a major rally, the Dail overwhelmingly passed an opposition motion demanding action of evictions and rents, increased investment in public housing and the creation of a legal Right to Housing. That motion also remains unrealised and we are now calling for its full implementation. Our campaign for 2019 is focused on delivering these measures and ensuring that citizens secure a Right to Housing.[5]

Anthony Flynn, a founder member of Inner City Helping Homeless and representative of the National Homeless & Housing Coalition, told the press conference that

> The motion that was passed in the Dail in October to implement a Right to Housing as well as action against evictions and increases in rental prices across the country hasn't yet been implemented by government. We intend to take the Raise the Roof campaign across

the country as the homeless and housing crisis impacts everyone, from students looking for accommodation to pensioners evicted from the private rental market. This is a national emergency with 4,000 children living in emergency accommodation. These children need homes built on public lands to properly develop and live normal lives. While official homeless figures sit just under the 10,000 mark we know that the real figure is much higher and with 50,000 mortgages in arrears we need immediate action from the government before the situation worsens – and we need the people of Ireland to join us in demanding a fairer country for all.[6]

Just like all its predecessors, today's housing campaign intends either to force a change of policy from the current Government or force a change of Government to ensure that the growing number of people left behind by Fine Gael and Fianna Fáil's failed housing policies have their housing needs met.

There has never been a better time to force a fundamental shift in our housing system. But it will take levels of mobilisation not seen since the Right to Water movement in 2014 and 2015 or the Fairer, Better Way campaign of 2010. It will require a broad-based, civil society-led campaign just like Marriage Equality and Together for Yes.

It will require not thousands, but tens of thousands of people to mobilise in towns and villages and cities across the State. It will need a level of pressure on politicians and prospective Councillors, TDs and MEPs during the elections campaigns that will arrive in the coming months.

And it will require a greater number of progressive politicians committed to radical policy, not because it is electorally expedient to advocate such change, but because of a sincere and genuine belief that that is what it will take to rebuild our housing system into one that functions in the interest of the many not just the few.

The year 2019 can and must be the year that we force a break with the failed policy consensus that has dominated Government thinking since the end of the 1980s. It can and must be the year in which we put our housing system on a course that over the coming decade will undo the damage of recent years and address the deeper structural weaknesses that the system inherited from earlier generations.

But mass mobilisation will be in vain if we do not have a coherent, credible and costed plan that sets out how, over a period of time, our dysfunctional housing system can be replaced with something truly better.

At the centre of all of our efforts must be the right to a home, for all people to be able to access secure, appropriate and affordable accommodation, that meets their social, economic and cultural needs and aspirations. For this to happen, public housing is the answer. Public housing on a scale not seen before in the history of this State.

This will require real ambition, to fundamentally change how we think about our housing system and the role Government must play to ensure that it serves all of the people.

Nye Bevan's Vision

In the aftermath of the Second World War, in a country whose housing stock was literally reduced to rubble from aerial bombardment, whose economy was in ruins and whose housing system had for decades been dominated by a *laissez faire* economic model that left hundreds of thousands in the squalor of slums, the newly appointed

Minister for Health and Housing confronted an impossible reality with a singular determination to meet people's needs through bold and ambitious Government intervention.

Aneurin Bevan is widely known for his pivotal role in the creation of the British National Health Service. The NHS is not only Britain's most popular and successful Government institution but it has provided others with a model for guaranteeing people health care on the basis of need and not ability to pay, that reduced health inequalities and provided world class health outcomes.

What is less well known is Nye Bevan's response to the housing crisis. His approach was exactly the same, and were it not for detractors within his own party and changes made by subsequent Conservative and Labour Governments, it may well have come to pass.

But notwithstanding his inability to fully realise his vision for public housing, it is as relevant today as it was then. In a landmark speech to the House of Commons during the passage of his Housing Bill in 1949 he outlined that vision:

I believe that one of the reasons why modern nations have not been able to solve their housing problems is that they have looked upon houses as commodities to be bought and sold and not as a social service to be provided. Housing experts ... are coming increasingly to recognise that the building industry cannot, in fact, be mobilised to meet the needs for modern housing in a modern industrial nation merely by leaving it to the laws of supply and demand.

A house is far too complex a product of modern society to be left to unplanned initiative. Therefore, it is essential that the State should take a hand in the provision of this modern necessity and do so by making housing a service. That can only be accomplished by reposing it in the custody of a public authority. This is especially the case where there is competition for houses. Only a public authority can choose between the relative claims of different applicants for houses. That cannot be done by private persons acting upon private enterprise only.

I believe, in the view of most people, it was entirely undesirable that on modern housing estates only one type of citizen should live ... if we are to enable citizens to lead a full life, if they are each to be aware of the problems of their neighbours, then they should be all drawn from the different sections of the community and we should try to introduce in our modern villages what was always the lovely feature of English and Welsh villages, where the doctor, the grocer, the butcher and farm labourer all lived in the same street. I believe that is essential for the full life of a citizen ... I believe it leads to the enrichment of every member of the community to live in communities of that sort.[7]

Bevan also understood that vibrant and sustainable communities needed dwellings built to the highest possible standards, giving working families the space and facilities to live a comfortable life.

At a time when much of the public focus was on the need to increase housing output to meet post-war demand for returning soldiers and their families, the Minister rightly focused as much on standards, believing that he would be judged not on the quantity of houses built under his stewardship but on their quality. In opposition to the maximum unit size of 69sq m permissible for Council houses under the previous Government, Bevan insisted on a minimum unit size of 88sq m. He also argued that homes for working families should have two toilets and bathrooms, not as a luxury but as a necessity.

Despite enormous pressure from colleagues and the opposition to reduce standards in order to increase output, Bevan stood firm arguing that such a course of action was 'the coward's way out' and that doing so would be 'a cruel thing to do. After all, people will have to live in and among these houses for many years.'[8] He also resisted attempts to resort to short-term modular building systems again on the grounds of maintaining standards. However, he was a strong advocate of using new building technologies that could meet minimum standards.

As Britain attempted to get to grips with the massive post-war need for housing there was a debate on what was the best delivery mechanism for his public house building programme. In opposition to calls for the creation of a statewide Housing Corporation he insisted that Local Councils be equipped with the finances and staff to build hundreds of thousands of homes. Former Labour Party MP and Leader Michael Foot in his biography of Bevan said that the Minister believed that 'housing cried aloud for a democratic organization' and that, Local Councillors being accountable to those most in need of houses then, Local Government was the most appropriate level at which decisions of what houses to build and where to build them should be made.[9]

The radical housing Minister's achievements were considerable. In 1946 the total number of new houses built was 55,400; this increased under Bevan's tenure to

139,690 in 1947, 227,616 in 1948 and 284,230 in 1948. While his Labour and Conservative successors outdid this level of construction they did so at the expense of standards and size and without the rate of growth achieved in the immediate post-war years.[10]

Nye Bevan's vision for public housing was broad, humane and inclusive. It sought to guarantee the right to housing not only of the most vulnerable in society but of working people generally, through the direct provision of high-quality, socially mixed, publicly funded and managed housing. That Bevan's vision was narrowed and contorted by many of his successors, and this was in turn used to justify the assault on public housing first by the Conservative administrations of Margaret Thatcher and then the Labour Governments of Tony Blair, should not blind us to the value of its original idea.

Bevan faced a challenge greater than those of our time but by combining that vision with a determination to deliver real change for working people he and his colleagues improved the quality of life for hundreds of thousands of people, guaranteeing them access to secure, appropriate and affordable homes. In doing so they set a standard for those of us serious about meeting housing need today.

We should embrace his vision and modernise it for the twenty-first century. Today our public housing should not only meet Bevan's high standards but exceed them. They should be built to the highest possible environmental standards, with the most efficient use of energy and the lowest possible carbon emissions. They should include beautiful, iconic buildings designed by the very best architects and built by trades persons who value their craft. With meaningful connections to their historical, cultural and ecological context.

Hatert Tower

If you think this is just a pipe dream take a look at what some other countries are doing. Nijmegen is a city of 750,000 people in the Netherlands on the border with Germany. As part of a country-wide social housing regeneration programme, new iconic public housing projects were built on vacant land alongside the refurbishment of existing older stock. Designed by 24H Architecture, Hatert Tower is a thirteen-story social housing development with a primary care centre on the ground floor and seventy-one apartments ranging from 84sq m to 109sq m. Built to high environmental standards, with an iconic design and incredible views of the city, it was awarded the Best Public Architecture Prize in 2012 following a public vote. The tenants come from the public housing lists, the rent is controlled, and at €12.5 million for the building and €1,000 per sq m for the apartments it was delivered at a cost that would be the envy of any Irish builder. If our Dutch neighbours can do this there is simply no reason that we can't.

Our housing system is at tipping point. If left to itself and to those responsible for its dysfunction it will tip back in the direction of the status quo, with all the structural imbalances and inequalities that go with it. The result will be ever growing numbers of people without access to appropriate, secure and affordable accommodation.

But if all those committed to real change come together, all those directly affected by our dysfunctional housing system and all those unaffected but who want to do right by those that are, then something else might just happen.

If together we Raise the Roof on the streets, in our schools and colleges, in the mainstream and independent media, across our places of work and leisure, in Councils and parliaments, then we have the numbers and the power to tip the balance in the other direction. If we can build a movement, united and strong, we can force a radical change in direction. A direction that puts human need ahead of financial gain. That values rights more than profits. And ensures, through the building and maintaining of a functioning housing system, that every single person has a place they can call home.

The Promise of the Democratic Programme

In his speech on the 100th anniversary of the inaugural meeting of the First Dáil Éireann President of Ireland Michael D. Higgins laid down a challenge. He told a special Oireachtas sitting of TDs, Senators, MPs and MEPs from every county in Ireland that

> The First Dáil proclaimed no narrow freedom, nor any stunted liberty for the revolutionary Irish republic. In that most revolutionary of documents … the Democratic Programme, the deputies assembled in the Mansion House one hundred years ago proclaimed that

> > We declare in the words of the Irish Republican Proclamation the right of the people of Ireland to the ownership of Ireland, and to the unfettered control of Irish destinies to be indefeasible, and in the language of our first President, Pádraig Mac Piarais, we declare that the Nation's sovereignty extends not only to all men and women of the Nation, but to all its material possessions, the Nation's soil and all its resources, all the wealth and all the wealth-producing processes within the

Nation, and with him we reaffirm that all right to private property must be subordinated to the public right and welfare.

The Programme clearly stated the duties and obligations of the new republic to its people, with these words:

It shall be the first duty of the Government of the Republic to make provision for the physical, mental and spiritual well-being of the children, to secure that no child shall suffer hunger or cold from lack of food, clothing or shelter, but that all shall be provided with the means and facilities requisite for their proper education and training, as citizens of a free and Gaelic Ireland.

In the Democratic Programme of the First Dáil, the ideals of Connolly found expression through reference to the words of Pádraig Mac Piarais in the Proclamation, an ideal of national freedom that included the dream and achievement of economic and social justice.

In the spirit of the movements which inspired both men, it is not simply utopian. It is emancipatory in its language, and programmatic and systemic in its vision. It is possible to trace a connection in the text from the Constitution of the Citizen Army through James Connolly to the Proclamation and on to the Democratic Programme as it would come to be known.

In place of fear, the Democratic Programme offered hope. In place of self-interest, it demanded duty. In place of injustice, it mandated equality. For our forebears were not merely opening a legislative assembly, they were founding a new nation, one capable of articulating and vindicating the rights and aspirations of the Irish people.[11]

The President then challenged those of us in the room to respond to the problems of today, including our housing emergency, according to the spirit and the letter of the Democratic Programme. He said:

> The destiny of our country, the fate of our Irish revolution, now lies in the hands of this generation of Irishwomen and Irishmen. It falls to us, the Irish people, to forge a renewed vision of Irish freedom in the world today. It is happening with a recognition of the power of creativity in arts, science, peace-keeping and shared global concern.
>
> The same challenges that confronted the revolutionary generation still abide with us today.
>
> We struggle to meet the needs of all of our people, even as our republic remains marred by inequalities in power, wealth, income and opportunity. Poverty subsists amidst plenty, even as we fail to provide some of our citizens with the basic elements of a dignified existence within our republic – housing, healthcare, education, support for those with particular needs.[12]

The destiny of our country, its economy and society and its housing system, is indeed in our hands. So let's reshape it, based on principles of justice, equality and solidarity and in so doing ensure that secure, appropriate and affordable accommodation is available for all.

Endnotes

Movement 1

1 O'Connell (2007) p4
2 Ibid. p4
3 Ibid. p5
4 Norris (2016) pp26–30
5 Kenna (2011) pp28–9
6 Ferriter (2005) p51
7 Ibid. p64
8 Ibid. p64
9 O'Connell (2007) p6
10 Kenna (2011) p22
11 Ferriter (2011) p52
12 Kenna (2011) p24
13 Ferriter (2005) p52
14 O'Connell (2007) p10
15 Kenna (2011) p34
16 Ferriter (2005) p160
17 Kenna (2011) p35
18 Ferriter (2005) p319
19 https://www.oireachtas.ie/en/debates/debate/dail/1923-05-04/10/?highlight%5B0%5D=cole&highlight%5B1%5D=william&highlight%5B2%5D=housing&highlight%5B3%5D=houses&highlight%5B4%5D=housing
20 Ibid. p319
21 O'Connell (2007) p25
22 Ibid. p20
23 Dublin Civic Survey 1925 quoted in O'Connell (2007) p21
24 O'Connell (2007) p20
25 Ibid. p27
26 Democratic Programme of the First Dáil 1919

27   Ferriter (2005) p319
28   O'Connell (2007) p29
29   Ibid. p29
30   Lee (1989) p193
31   Lee (1989) p193
32   Quoted in O'Connell (2007) p89
33   Ferriter (2005) p398
34   Ibid. p399
35   Lee (1989) p309
36   Ibid. p497
37   Keogh (1994) p197
38   Norris (ND) p7
39   Kenna (2011) p42
40   Norris (2016) p130
41   Patterson (2002) p113
42   Keogh (1994) p268
43   Ibid. p268
44   Ibid. p270
45   Kenna (2011) p50
46   Norris (2016) p151
47   Based on an account of the episode in Keogh (1994) p272

Movement 2

1   Norris (2013) p15
2   Ibid. pp17, 18
3   Norris (2011) p7
4   Ibid. p12
5   Department of Environment (1991)
6   Norris (2016) p181
7   O'Connell (2007) pp51, 52
8   Ibid. p110
9   Ibid. p43
10   Norris (2011) p13
11   Norris (2013) p17
12   Ibid. p17
13   Ibid. pp16, 19
14   Ibid. p19
15   Norris (2016) p167
16   Ibid. p120

17 Norris (2013) p20
18 Collins (2018) p48
19 Ibid. p32
20 Ibid. p34
21 NESC (1988) p13
22 Ibid. pp38, 39
23 Ibid. p62
24 Department of Environment (1991) p5
25 Ibid. p6
26 Ibid. p10
27 Ibid. p10
28 Ibid. p11
29 Ibid. p22
30 Ibid. p23
31 O'Connell (2007) p110
32 Department of Housing, Planning and local Government website
33 Housing Agency (2011) p6
34 Norris (2011) p16
35 Norris (2013) p21
36 Department of Environment (1995)
37 Centre for Housing Research (2006) p51
38 Parliamentary Question 47442/17 answered on 9.11.17
39 Drudy (2005) p11
40 Ibid. p23
41 Ibid. p51
42 NESC (2004) p77
43 Ibid. p72
44 Ryan-Collins (2018) p54
45 Ibid. p55
46 Ibid. p55
47 Norris (2016) p226
48 Ryan-Collins (1018) p60
49 NESC (2004) p3
50 Ibid. p3
51 Ibid. p17
52 Ibid. p91
53 Ibid. p29
54 Department of Environment (2005) p1
55 Ibid. pp2, 4
56 Department of Housing, ESB connection statistics
57 NESC (2004) p17

58   Norris (2016) p119
59   Quoted in Drudy and Punch (2005) p101
60   Ibid. p102
61   Lewis (2019) p75
62   Department of Environment (2007) p3
63   Department of Public Expenditure and Reform (2017) and Department of Housing (various)
64   Housing Agency (2013) and PQ 47442/17 answered on 9.11.17
65   Department of Housing website
66   Department of Environment (2011) p2
67   Ibid. p2
68   Ibid. p2
69   Department of Environment (2014) pv
70   Ibid. ppiii, iv
71   Department of Housing website (various dates)
72   Irish Times 4.11.15
73   Houses of the Oireachtas (2016) p2
74   Ibid. p5
75   Ibid. p5
76   Ibid. p5
77   Ibid. p5
78   Central Bank website (2016 Q2 mortgage arrears and repossession statistics)
79   Ibid.
80   Ibid.
81   Houses of the Oireachtas (2016) p6
82   Ibid. p6
83   Ibid. p6
84   Ibid. p6
85   Quoted in Irish Times, 17.6.16
86   Fianna Fáil (2016)
87   Programme for Partnership Government (2016) p20
88   Ibid. p20
89   Ibid. p32
90   Department of Housing, *Rebuilding Ireland* (2016) p5
91   Ibid. pp6, 7
92   Ibid. p8
93   Ibid. p35
94   Ibid. p36
95   Ibid. p46 & PQ 609,624, Ref: 43835/17, 32992/15 answered on 17/10/17

96 Ibid. pp47, 48
97 Ibid. p62
98 Ibid. p62
99 Ibid. p59
100 Ibid. pp75–6
101 https://www.irishtimes.com/opinion/conor-skehan-housing-plan-shows-welcome-signs-of-joined-up-thinking-1.2728840
102 https://www.irishtimes.com/opinion/michelle-norris-action-plan-must-deliver-on-social-housing-targets-1.2727577
103 Department of Housing website (various dates)
104 Housing Agency (2017)
105 Calculated by combining Summary of Social Housing Assessment numbers from Housing Agency (2017) with HAP and RAS figures from Department of Housing (various dates)
106 Daft.ie website (various dates)
107 Daft.ie (2017 Q2)
108 RTB.ie website (various dates)
109 Ibid.
110 Ibid.
111 https://www.thejournal.ie/help-to-buy-2-4323270-Jan2019/
112 Oireachtas.ie, Dáil Debates, 14.12.16
113 Department of Housing, 3rd Quarterly Progress Report on *Rebuilding Ireland* (May 2017)
114 *Irish Examiner*, 20.7.16
115 Oireachtas, 14.6.17
116 Ibid.
117 CSO (2018) https://www.cso.ie/en/methods/governmentaccounts/classificationdecisions/classificationofapprovedhousingbodies/
118 PQs 46002 & 46003 answered on 7.11.18
119 https://www.kildarestreet.com/wrans/?id=2019-01-15a.11&s=Repair+and+lease+speaker%3A407#g12.q
120 PQ 36333/18 answered on 7.9.18
121 Department of Housing National Vacant Housing Reuse Strategy 2018–2021 (2018)
122 PQs 3615 & 3616 answered on 24.1.18
123 Oireachtas Housing Committee, 26.9.18
124 Department of Housing website (various dates)
125 Oireachtas Housing Committee, 8.11.18
126 Ibid.
127 Oireachtas Housing Committee, 17.5.18
128 Daft.ie (various dates)

129 RTB.ie (various dates)
130 Housing Agency (figures provided to author)
131 The Journal.ie, 16.6.18
132 https://www.housing.gov.ie/housing/government-launches-eu125bn-land-development-agency-build-150000-new-homes
133 https://www.businesspost.ie/politics/housing-taking-toll-missing-minister-murphy-430803
134 *The Irish Mail on Sunday*, 6.1.19
135 Ibid. p6
136 Oireachtas, 25.9.18
137 Ibid.
138 https://www.ictu.ie/press/2018/09/05/trade-unions-housing-advocates-community-campaign/
139 Ibid.
140 Ibid.
141 Sirr et al (2014)
142 Department of Public Expenditure and Reform (2017)
143 *The Irish Times*, 22.6.18

Movement 3

1 Kirby & Murphy (2007), Kirby (2002), Kirby (2010)
2 http://eprintsprod.nuim.ie/1133/1/MMMurphy_and_Kirby.pdf
3 Ryan-Collins (2018) p87
4 Ibid. p87
5 Ibid. p93
6 http://www.constitutionalconvention.ie/AttachmentDownload.ashx?mid=5333bbe7-a9b8-e311-a7ce-005056a32ee4
7 *The Irish Times*, 22.2.14
8 Ibid.
9 http://www.mercylaw.ie/_fileupload/Right%20to%20Housing%20Report.pdf
10 https://www.oireachtas.ie/en/debates/debate/committee_on_housing_and_homelessness/2016-05-10/5/
11 Report on the Committee on Housing and Homelessness (2016) p138
12 https://www.oireachtas.ie/en/debates/debate/dail/2017-09-28/9/
13 https://www.oireachtas.ie/en/debates/debate/joint_committee_on_housing_planning_and_local_government/2018-06-12/3/
14 Ibid.

15   Irish Human Rights and Equality Commission press release, 10.12.18

16   https://www.nerinstitute.net/download/pdf/irelands_housing_emergency_time_for_a_game_changer.pdf?issuusl=ignore

17   https://www.ocualann.ie/

18   https://www.independent.ie/opinion/comment/paul-melia-with-so-much-land-effectively-owned-by-the-citizens-a-joinedup-approach-is-now-urgently-needed-37484447.html

19   https://www.dublininquirer.com/2018/02/14/mick-michelle-and-anna-our-housing-policy-is-built-on-a-false-and-dangerous-premise

20   Fahey (1997) p267

21   Ibid. p250

22   Ibid. p251

23   Fahey (1997), Atkinson (2016), Sautkina et al (2012), Carnegie et al (2018)

24   NESC (2004) p50

25   ESRI (June 2018) pp1, 2

26   Figures provided to the author from the Residential Tenancies Board

27   https://www.communityfoundation.ie/images/uploads/research-reports/The_Future_Of_Council_Housing_(Norris_Hayden).pdf

28   https://ec.europa.eu/eurostat/documents/1015035/8683865/Advice-2018-IE-Sector-classification-Approved-Housing-Bodies.pdf/4813b7be-a51b-4952-bbb2-46906aacbbdd

29   https://www.irishmirror.ie/news/irish-news/politics/sinn-fein-bill-calling-developers-13664400

30   Figures provided to the author by the Residential Tenancies Board

31   Department of Housing, *Rebuilding Ireland* (2016) p72

32   https://www.housing.gov.ie/sites/default/files/publications/files/strategy_for_the_rental_sector_final.pdf

33   Ibid.

34   http://noac.ie/wp-content/uploads/2018/09/NOAC-Performance-Indicators-Report-2017.pdf

35   https://pdf.cso.ie/www/pdf/20181109085126_New_Dwelling_Completions_Q3_2018_full.pdf

36   https://www.irishtimes.com/news/social-affairs/housing-needs-blown-out-of-proportion-1.3339173 & https://www.housing.eolasmagazine.ie/the-challenge-of-housing-obsolescence/

37   http://www.sinnfein.ie/files/2018/AlternativeBudget2019_web.pdf

38   Department of Environment (1995)

39   Fahey (1999), Norris (2014)
40   https://www.irishtimes.com/opinion/terrible-legacy-of-corrupt-quarryvale-rezoning-1.489779
41   http://www.supremecourt.ie/supremecourt/sclibrary3.nsf/(WebFiles)/312ADADEE5E1311F802575F300333DEA/$FILE/Planning_%5B2000%5D%202%20IR%20321.htm
42   https://www.irishtimes.com/news/social-affairs/dalkey-developer-seeks-516-400-per-social-housing-apartment-1.3213313
43   Ryan-Collins et al. (2017) p205
44   https://www.irishtimes.com/opinion/mick-wallace-how-to-stop-the-developers-sitting-on-land-1.3550084
45   https://www.irishexaminer.com/breakingnews/ireland/ireland-worst-performing-european-country-at-tackling-climate-change-891121.html
46   https://www.kildarestreet.com/wrans/?id=2019-01-16a.548&s=Near+zero+energy+speaker%3A407#g549.q
47   https://www.cso.ie/en/releasesandpublications/er/dber/domesticbuildingenergyratingsquarter42018/
48   Citizens Assembly, Third Report, 18.4.18
49   https://www.oireachtas.ie/en/debates/debate/joint_committee_on_housing_planning_and_local_government/2018-11-06/3/
50   https://www.ihrec.ie/app/uploads/2018/06/Discrimination-and-Inequality-in-Housing-in-Ireland..pdf
51   https://www.ihrec.ie/app/uploads/2018/06/Discrimination-and-Inequality-in-Housing-in-Ireland..pdf

Coda

1   https://www.thetimes.co.uk/edition/ireland/dublin-housing-crisis-will-take-years-to-fix-says-council-boss-ft2pn75fw
2   https://redcresearch.ie/wp-content/uploads/2018/10/SBP-October-2018-Poll-Report-Presidential-and-General-Election.pdf
3   *Irish Daily Mail*, 9.1.19
4   Clapham (2019) p5
5   https://www.ictu.ie/press/2019/01/24/raise-the-roof-launches-major-campaign-on-right-to/
6   Ibid.
7   Hansard, 16.3.1949
8   Foot (1997) p274
9   Ibid. p269

10   Ibid. p278
11   https://president.ie/en/media-library/speeches/address-on-the-
     100th-anniversary-of-the-inaugural-meeting-of-the-first-dail-
     eireann
12   Ibid.

Bibliography

Atkinson, Rowland, Keith Jacobs. (2016) *House, Home and Society*. Palgrave.

Boughton, John. (2018) *Municipal Dreams: The Rise and Fall of Council Housing*. Verso.

Carnegie, Anna et al. (2018) 'Tenure Mixing to Combat Public Housing Stigmatization'. In *Cities Journal* ed. 79.

Centre for Housing Research. (2006) *Supplementary Welfare Allowance, Rent Supplement: Implications for the Implementation of the Rental Accommodation Scheme*.

Clapham, David. (2019) *Remaking Housing Policy: An International Study*. Routledge.

Committee on the Price of Building Land. (1972) *Report to the Minister for Local Government*.

Committee on Housing and Homelessness. (2016) *Report of the Committee on Housing and Homelessness*. Oireachtas.

Corrigan, Eoin et al. (2018a) *Exploring Affordability in the Irish Housing Market*, Working Paper no. 593. ESRI.

Corrigan, Eoin, Dorothy Watson. (2018b) *Social Housing in the Irish Housing Market*, Working Paper no. 594. ESRI.

Davitt, Michael. (1904) *The Fall of Feudalism in Ireland: Or, the Story of the Land League Revolution*. Harper and Brothers Publishers.

Department of Environment. (1991) *A Plan for Social Housing*.

Department of Environment. (2005) *Housing Policy Framework, Building Sustainable Communities*.

Department of Environment. (2007) *Delivering Homes, Sustaining Communities*.

Department of Environment. (2011) *Housing Policy Statement*.

Department of Environment. (2014) *Social Housing Strategy 2020, Support, Supply and Reform*.

Department of Housing. (2016) *Action Plan for Housing and Homelessness.*

Department of Housing. (2017) *Second Report on Implementation of the National Housing Strategy for People with a Disability.*

Department of Public Expenditure and Reform. (2017) *Analysis of Current Expenditure on Housing Supports.*

Drudy, P.J., Michael Punch. (2005) *Out of Reach: Inequalities in the Irish Housing System.* TASC.

Dunphy, Richard. (1995) *The Making of Fianna Fáil: Power in Ireland 1923–1948.* Clarendon Press.

Fahey, Tony ed. (1997) *Social Housing in Ireland: A Study of Success, Failure and Lessons Learned.* Oak Tree Press.

Fahey, Tony, Michelle Norris. (2011) *From Asset Based Welfare to Welfare Housing? The Changing Function of Social Housing in Ireland.* UCD Press.

Ferriter, Diarmaid. (2005) *The Transformation of Ireland, 1900–2000.* Profile Books.

Foot, Michael. (1997) *Aneurin Bevan.* Indigo.

Gray, Neil ed. (2018) *Rent and its Discontents: A Century of Struggle.* Rowman and Littlefield.

Hanley, Lynsey. (2017) *Estates: An Intimate History.* Granta Books.

Housing Agency. (2018) *Summary of Social Housing Assessments 2018.*

Irish Human Rights and Equality Commission, ESRI. (2018) *Discrimination and Inequality in Housing in Ireland.*

Kenna, Padraic. (2011) *Housing Law, Rights and Policy.* Clarus Press.

Keogh, Dermot. (1994) *Twentieth-Century Ireland: Nation and State.* Gill and Macmillan.

Kirby, Peadar. (2002) *The Celtic Tiger in Distress: Growth with Inequality in Ireland.* Palgrave.

Kirby, Peadar, Mary Murphy. (2007) *Ireland as a Competition State.* IPEG Papers.

Kirby, Peadar. (2010) *Celtic Tiger in Collapse: Explaining the Weaknesses of the Irish Model.* Palgrave.

Lee, J.J. (1989) *Ireland, 1912–1985: Politics and Society.* Cambridge University Press.

Lewis, Eddie. (2019) *Social Housing Policy in Ireland: New Directions.* Institute of Public Administration.

MacDermott, Eithne. (1998) *Clann na Poblachta.* Cork University Press.

McCabe, Conor. (2011) *Sins of the Father: Tracing the Decisions that Shaped the Irish Economy*. The History Press.

Minton, Anna. (2010) *Big Capital, Who Is London For?* Penguin.

Madden, David, Peter Marcuse. (2016) *In Defence of Housing*. Verso.

Mulholland, Marc. (2000) *Northern Ireland at the Crossroads*. Macmillan Press.

Mullins, David, Peter Shanks. (2016) *Housing in Northern Ireland*. Chartered Institute of Housing.

Murphy, Mary, Michelle Millar. (ND) *The NESC Developmental Welfare State: A Glass Half Empty or a Glass Half Full?*

National Economic and Social Council. (1988) *A Review of Housing Policy*.

National Economic and Social Council. (2004) *Housing in Ireland, Performance and Policy*.

National Economic and Social Council. (2014) *Social Housing at the Crossroads: Possibilities for Investment, Provision and Cost Rental*.

Norris, Michelle. (2013) *Varieties of Home Ownership: Ireland's Transition from a Socialised to a Marketised Policy Regime*. UCD Press.

Norris, Michelle ed. (2014) *Social Housing, Disadvantage and Neighbourhood Liveability: Ten Years of Change in Social Housing Neighbourhoods*. Routledge.

Norris, Michelle. (2016) *Property, Family and the Irish Welfare State*. Palgrave.

Norris, Michelle, Aideen Hayden. (2018) *The Future of Council Housing: An Analysis of the Financial Sustainability of Local Authority Provided Social Housing*. The Community Foundation for Ireland.

O'Connell, Cathal. (2007) *The State and Housing in Ireland: Ideology, Policy and Practice*. Nova.

Ó Riain, Seán. (2014) *The Rise and Fall of Ireland's Celtic Tiger: Liberalism, Boom and Bust*. Cambridge University Press.

Paris, Chris. (2001) *Housing in Northern Ireland – and Comparisons with the Republic of Ireland*. Chartered Institute of Housing.

Patterson, Henry. (2002) *Ireland Since 1939*. Oxford University Press.

Ryan-Collins, Josh, Toby Lloyd, Laurie Macfarlane. (2017) *Rethinking the Economics of Land and Housing*. Zed.

Ryan-Collins, Josh. (2018) *Why Can't You Afford a Home?* Polity.

Sautkina, Elena et al. (2012) 'Missed Evidence on Mixed Tenure Effects'. In *Housing Studies* Vol. 27, No. 6. Routledge.

Sirr, Lorcan ed. (2014) *Renting in Ireland: The Social, Voluntary and Private Sectors*. Institute of Public Administration.

Supreme Court of Ireland. (2000) In the matter of Article 26 of the Constitution and in the matter of Part V of the *Planning and Development Bill*, 1999. (S.C. no. 184 of 2000)

Sweeney, Eamonn. (2010) *Down Down Deeper and Down: Ireland in the 70s & 80s*. Gill and Macmillan.

Thomas-Symonds, Nicklaus. (2018) *Nye: The Political Life of Aneurin Bevan*. I.B. Tauris.

Index

national planning and regional
balance, 216–18, 220
National Planning Network as
statutory plan, the, 218, 219
National Spatial Strategy and
decentralisation, the, 217
National Women's Council, the,
133, 134
NDP (National Development Plan),
the, 171, 195, 196, 200, 202,
219
Nearly Zero Energy Building
regulations, 226, 227, 228
negative equity, 183
neoliberalism, 48, 53–5, 138, 145,
146, xvi
NESC (National Economic and
Social Council), the, 67, 73,
88–9, 130, 218, 220; and *The
Developmental Welfare State*
(report), 79, 108, 145, 149,
166; *Housing in Ireland* (2004
report), 70–2, 84, 109, 148,
149, 161, 169, 180, 181–2,
217; review on housing policy,
56–7, 58, 75, 78, 96; *Urban
Development Land* (report),
221
Nevin Economic Research Institute,
the, 161, 174
NHS (National Health Service),
the, 247
*Ninth Progress Report of the All-
Party Oireachtas Committee on
the Constitution* (report), 221
no confidence motion in Eoghan
Murphy, 132–3
non-market component in public
housing provision, 180–1
non-nationals and access to
housing, 236

non-subsidised public housing,
160–1, 163, 179
non-subsidised rental tenants, 91,
186
Noonan, Michael, 92, 112, 141
Norris, Michelle, 34–5, 40, 44, 48,
51, 63, 75–6, 107, 233
not-for-profit and social housing, 60,
72, 119, 141, 159, 161, 175–6
Nunan, Sheila, 133–4, 244
nZEB (Near Zero Energy Building)
obligations, 227, 228, 230

Ó Cualann Co-Housing Alliance,
162
Ó Riain, Seán, 81
O'Brien, Darragh, 133
O'Connell, Cathal, 18, 137
O'Connell, Hugh, 131
O'Connor, Fr Ferghal, 42
O'Connor, Orla, 134
off-balance sheet delivery
mechanisms, 175–6
Oireachtas Committee on Housing
and Homelessness, the, 102,
118, 123, 124, 126, 129, 130,
156, 211–13, 233
Oireachtas Disability Group, the,
234
O'Riordan, Michael, 42
O'Sullivan, Eoin, 123–4
O'Sullivan, Jan, 83
Outlook (TV programme), 42
over-expenditure on the rent
supplement, 64, 74
over-reliance on the private market,
12
overcrowded accommodation, 24,
33, 190, 236
owner occupiers (*see*
homeownership)